THE PRINCIPLES
OF
SEDUCTION

THE PRINCIPLES OF SEDUCTION

How To Get Another Person To Fall In Love With You

G. Clayton Viddler

PEDESTAL PRESS   NEW YORK

Published by Pedestal Press, Inc.
P.O. Box 6093, Yorkville Station
New York, New York 10128

Grateful acknowledgment is made for permission to
use material from the following copyrighted works:
The Art and Science of Love by Albert Ellis. Copyright
1960 by The Institute for Rational Living, Inc. Re-
printed by permission of Albert Ellis, Ph.D.
Sexual Attraction and Love by Richard Centers. Copyright 1975 by Charles C. Thomas, Publisher. Courtesy
of Charles C. Thomas, Publisher, Springfield, Illinois.
Falling in Love by Francisco Alberoni, translated by
Lawrence Venturi. Translation copyright 1983 by
Lawrence Venturi. Reprinted by permission of Random House Inc.
About Love by Robert C. Solomon. Copyright 1988 by
Robert C. Solomon. Reprinted by permission of Simon
and Schuster.
The author also wishes to thank Revista de Occidente
en Alianza Editorial, Madrid, for permission to trans-
late excerpts from *Estudios Sobre el Amor* by Jose Ortega
y Gasset: revised second edition, Copyright 1981

ISBN 0-9627602-6-9

Printed in the United States of America

CONTENTS

Acknowledgements 3
Introduction 7

PART I.   WHAT CAUSES LOVE

Chapter 1: Defining Love's Ingredients 13

Chapter 2: What the Other Person Experiences
When They Are In Love 21

Chapter 3: Love is a Way to Experience a
Form of Complete Fulfillment 32

Chapter 4: The Roots of Love 39

PART II.   A STRATEGY OF SEDUCTION

Chapter 5: The Technique of Seduction 55

Chapter 6: Uncovering Someone's Unique Worth 65

Chapter 7: Making Sure Your Affirmations Count 70

PART III. FINDING SOMEONE SPECIAL

Chapter 8: Knowing What You're Looking For 81

Chapter 9: Starting Out With The Right
Attitude 86

Chapter 10: Locating Someone Desirable 94

PART IV.   MAKING THE INITIAL CONTACT

Chapter 11: Approaching Men 103

Chapter 12: Approaching Women 113

Chapter 13: Confirming the Other's Gender Identity 121

PART V. HOW TO WIN A SPECIFIC INDIVIDUAL'S LOVE

Chapter 14: Developing Emotional Rapport   135

Chapter 15: Seducing Introverts   147

Chapter 16: Seducing Extroverts   164

Chapter 17: On the Brink of Love   183

Chapter 18: Identifying Another Person's Self-Ideal   189

Chapter 19: Validating Your Partner's Self-Ideal   195

PART VI. CONCLUSION

Chapter 20: Doing it Good   209

Chapter 21: The Fruits of Seduction   218

APPENDIX. UNRAVELING THE MYSTERY OF LOVE   223

Section 1: Philosophical Anticipations of
            Today's Concept   224

Section 2: The Origins of a Scientific
            Perspective   232

Section 3: The Self-Ideal: Fact or Illusion   245

Notes   259

Index   265

ACKNOWLEDGMENTS

Writing is one part gestation and at least twice as many parts rewriting. During this process, I have benefited greatly from the advice of many people. Maron Waxman convinced me early on that what I thought was a finished product was really nothing but a beginning. In reworking that beginning, M. J. Abadie, Andrew Ludwig, and Shelagh Masline, three outstanding free lance editors, showed me how clarity and truth can coexist comfortably. In addition, the following people took time to read the manuscript, and made valuable suggestions which I have incorporated in the final text: Julie Farmer, Don Farley, Chris Nevradakis, Dr. James Carr, Robin Tasch, Linda and Harley Goldstrom, Dr. Roseanne Gotterbarn, and Dr. Lora Sporny. My brother Stephen Holing and his wife Linda provided unswerving encouragement; Linda also combed through each page and eliminated a host of grammatical glitches. Finally, throughout each stage of what has often seemed an unending process, my wife Deborah never lost faith that it would be properly completed. I have been able to persevere due to, and at times even revelled in, her trust.

INTRODUCTION

You, who in Cupid's rolls inscribe your name,
First seek an object worthy of your flame;
Then strive, with art, (their) mind to gain;
And last, provide your love may long remain.
On these three precepts all my work shall move:
These are the rules and principles of love.

OVID,
The Art of Love

INTRODUCTION

T his is a book for anyone seeking all the ardor and intimacy that can only be found in a passionate relationship, and who is ready to learn what it actually takes to achieve it. Are you still out there on the prowl in singles bars? Have you resorted to personal ads in the local newspaper? Are you sick and tired of blind dates? Is it time to curl up with a glass of wine, a box of tissues, and an old movie? Or do you presently have a partner who is basically admirable, but you know there's a vital spark missing between the two of you?

It doesn't have to be that way. Anyone can attain the love he or she wants if they go after it in the right way. Unfortunately, most people's thinking is muddled up in images of candy, candlelight and flowers. Not that there's anything wrong with those . . . but first things first. Let's get practical.

Winning someone's love is something that is going to involve the other person's inner feelings. They are not going to feel this way about you simply because Fate decided it's your lucky day. Another's love is always contingent on the way they react to how you relate to them. Obviously, then, the best approach you can take is to know beforehand *what has to go on in the other person's mind* that would lead them to react to *you* in that special way.

How do people fall in love? What has the greatest romantic impact on someone? Is it their favorite perfume, or your remembering their birthday? Let's not kid ourselves: these things only have a symbolical significance. But what is that deeper significance all about? We won't have to go into complicated considerations to find the answer. Scientific studies conducted over the past several decades have already done that for us.

During the last thirty to forty years social psychologists have been focusing their research efforts on finding the underlying motives of romantic behavior. And from the studies conducted so far there's been enough discovered to give us the basic answer to our question.

Basically, love arises when you relate to certain very specific components of another person's self-identity. More importantly, several researchers have pinpointed the exact ones which normally play the major role. These three components of a person's identity always come into play: *gender; social persona;* and the *self-ideal.*

This is a highly significant revelation. It means that evoking another person's love really involves a limited and understandable set of variables. Intentionally evoking someone's love boils down to identifying, and satisfying three specific parts of their self-identity. This simple knowledge can put you in a commanding position. It will allow you not only to foster the process of love, but also to avoid the many stumbling blocks that can keep anyone from getting the desired outcome.

Accordingly, the strategy we are going to use will be based on your getting a firm grasp of the factors that are responsible for causing people to fall in love. Given that love is something dependent on a limited set of components, all easily understood, this means it is something that *you can learn to master.*

After you've finished reading this book you are going to have a new and powerful option at your disposal. These pages will allow you to adopt an approach that can easily be put into practice, and that will be effective with almost anyone. No, this book is not going to provide you with recipes for magic potions, nor the exact wording for an irresistible pitch, but it will make a difference that *really* counts on the scales on which everyone's romantic fortunes are weighed.

The approach will be practical and straightforward. No mincing words — go out and get what you want, need, love — you're the boss of your own life, and can define your own goals and achieve them. All you need is some sense of how to go about it.

Are you prepared to find out how to do this? It takes only a short while to learn how. But this will be time well spent because there *is* a special someone for you, and this book will arm you with the knowledge to induce love in that person. The following chapters will empower you with the knowledge and ability to determine your own romantic future.

* * *

Let me reassure you that if any of this sounds complicated, that won't be the case. The contents of this book are both simple and workable. Actually the fundamental premise is something so intrinsically obvious that you've probably thought about it yourself. It's really quite simple — more a matter of seeing things you are already familiar with, but in a new and exciting way, and not incidently, one that can be truly *seductive*.

Focus your attention on what actually causes people to fall in love, and these pages will open up a whole new world for you — a world in which you can truly work a little magic and in fact become irresistible. And this applies whether you are male or female, because love happens to grip people of either sex in essentially the same way. In other words, it involves the same three components of personality in both men and women.

PART I

WHAT CAUSES LOVE

... we are taught that love should be completely selfless when in fact there is no emotion that has more to do with the self ... What should strike us is not the mystery but rather the very familiarity of love ... love is not a mysterious "union" of two otherwise separate and isolated selves but rather a special instance of the mutually defined creation of selves ... love is fundamentally the experience of redefining one's self in terms of the other.

ROBERT C. SOLOMON,
About Love

CHAPTER ONE

DEFINING LOVE'S INGREDIENTS

Until very recently we knew more about the forces that determine the motion of distant stars than about what's behind the mutual attraction felt between two people. But during the past few decades scientific researchers have made great strides in pinpointing the specific human needs that make love such a meaningful and necessary part of our life.

There's been a revolution in objectively understanding romantic behavior, and its links to three key aspects of our personalities. However, so far this new knowledge hasn't been made widely available to most people; it remains silently tucked away in scientific journals. Nevertheless, the fact that this information exists means that no one's prospects in this area have to stay solely subject to the dictates of fate. Since the findings uncovered by today's research actually reveal what it takes to get the love each of us legitimately desires, we no longer have to guess or bank on luck in our approach to love.

Unfortunately, though, these discoveries haven't made any national headlines yet. Nor have they worked their way into the popular literature on romantic relations. This is regrettable because a familiarity with these developments allows us to see the reality of love where before we may have seen only shadows. So I have spent the past several years reviewing everything that these investigations into love have uncovered. And throughout I've concentrated on extracting the scientific findings which have the greatest *practical* applications.

Instead of your having to accept Fate's stingy allotment of a fifty-fifty chance in your intimate relations, we can now put the pieces together in a way that will enable you to stack the principle odds in your own favor.

In order not to stray from our main objective, I have placed the detailed description of this scientific revolution in an appendix at the back of this book. Most readers have a pragmatic, concrete outlook, and are not as interested in a concept's background as they are in its applications. So we are going to keep as close to the practical as possible. However, anyone who prefers a solid grounding in the historical tradition which led to today's discoveries can turn to the Appendix before continuing.

* * *

Is it possible to make someone fall in love with us, if we want to? Listen to how one expert, Francesco Alberoni, describes the possibility of inducing love:

Yes. This is possible because there is always someone who is ready for love, who is ready to hurl himself into the all or nothing of a new life . . . It is possible . . . if, at the right moment, he meets a person who shows that she understands him profoundly, who encourages him and his desire for renewal ... Anyone can cause a person who is waiting for the summons to fall in love if she can make him hear the voice that calls him by name and tells him that his time has come, if she tells him that she is here to recognize the destiny that is his, if she makes out the signs of it on his face, his hands, in what he has done. She makes herself someone who embodies a certainty and calls him to her so that they can move beyond. Then he *recognizes himself* in her and falls in love.[1] (my italics)

While this beautiful description is definitely on target, it doesn't convey the kind of information that lends itself to being easily applied. Since our approach to seduction is going to involve addressing the specific factors which cause people to fall in love, a great deal depends on knowing *exactly* what to aim for. Our strategy will be effective only to the extent that our working concept explicitly states what happens in reality.

Fortunately a number of researchers have focused specifically on the most common denominators. Using experimental methods, psychologists have found that love arises from certain motives built into everyone's self-identity. This means that the kind of self-recognition Alberoni referred to above is not the kind people get from looking in a mirror. The self-recognition which directly causes a person to fall in love involves that person's self-identity. It is the sense of who and what they are, *as well as what they can be*, that causes this.

By exploring which aspects of personality are directly involved in starting the flow of romantic feelings, psychologists discovered that just three basic components of a person's identity are important: their *gender*; their *social persona*; and in more intimate contexts, their *ideal self*. These happen to be the most subjectively meaningful aspects of everyone's identity, our deepest sense of who we really are.

This is why these three variables have the highest impact on the deeply personal feelings that move a person to fall in love. Contrary to popular belief, love is not some ephemeral force that grips us from the outside. Rather, it is formed directly from needs that exist within each person's own psyche.

In keeping with this fundamental reality, the strategy we are going to develop in the rest of this book will primarily concentrate on the following three aspects of another person's self-identity:

1. Gender identity (masculine or feminine)
2. Social self-image (either introverted or extroverted)
3. Self-ideal (which usually has either a traditional or an unconventional cast)

* * *

To give you a general idea of the way these components of personality play a role in the birth of love, let's briefly look at how the first of them operates in these situations.

A story recounted by Heather T. Remoff in her book *Sexual Choice, A Woman's Decision*, clearly illustrates how a person's sense of "gender identity" can unwittingly trigger their romantic interest. The incident described by Remoff involved a woman friend who had recently fallen in love with a business associate. Curiously enough, what set the stage for this joyous event was the fact that Remoff's friend had just gotten over a bout of hepatitis. In Remoff's words:

> They had met to discuss business over dinner. Glenna ordered herself a drink (alcohol) and her companion, knowing her medical history, (*e.g.*, her recent hepatitis) swiftly, surely, and with absolute resolve cancelled her order and instructed the waitress to bring instead two club sodas. Glenna fumed and fretted (but) fell in love.[2]

Why did this affect Glenna's sense of gender identity? How was a romantic response stirred in her? In the first place, the man's decisive act implied he felt she needed to be protected. Considering her recent medical condition Glenna could hardly mistake the man's proper concern: alcohol and hepatitis don't mix. So rather than interpreting his assertiveness as an expression of "machismo," Glenna couldn't help feeling herself sheltered by the male's protectiveness.

But by relating to her in this distinctly masculine way, it also conveyed a personal assumption on his part, namely that a heterosexual context existed between them. His response not only made her feel sheltered but also truly feminine. Simply sensing that this aspect of herself — her femininity — had been confirmed is what moved Glenna to turn her attention from business to pleasure. Of course the thought that something exciting was about to happen was suggested by other things too. And we will go into those later.

But what initially made the prospect of pleasure stand out was that the situation had been immediately turned in a definite man-woman direction. Love always begins on the basis of how two people respond to certain specific aspects of each other's personalities. In this case, the confirmation Glenna found for her sense of gender opened her up to later confirmations of the other two major aspects of her identity. It didn't take long before they both knew that business was destined to wind up on the back burner whenever they got together again.

* * *

When you set out to win someone's love, it is largely your response to certain aspects of their *self-identity* that counts. Whether the other wears these on their sleeve, or keeps them under the surface, the way these particular facets of their identity fare with you during an encounter determines whether they are going to think of you as a potential lover.

Of course there can be any number of other things involved in a love relation which may momentarily be more pressing, or even of greater interest. Still, without qualification, the core of a person's identity is what has the most far-reaching implications for anyone who is undergoing this experience.

This is particularly the case when it comes to the more passionate and romantic forms of love. The degree of passion a person experiences builds within them in proportion to the specific aspects of their identity which you support when you are together. And romantic implications will emerge from the rhythm with which you provide this special kind of support.

Once a relationship has gained significance — once you have tapped the core of the three aspects of personality which make up your special someone's sense of identity — he or she will be ready and fully disposed to fall in love. As you gratify now one, now another of these particular parts of their identity, that person will come to feel that you find them very appealing. And no doubt you do!

Eventually this will also make them feel an increased sense of wholeness within themselves. In turn, since it's going to be *you* who's going to lead them to experience this form of inner wholeness, they will feel impelled to fall in love with you.

* * *

Love is based on three specific factors, and it comes into being on the basis of those three factors whether a person is aware of it or not. This means that rather than having to be a question of hit or miss, it is indeed possible to create romantic bonds by going for these particular aspects of your partner's personality.

The following chapters of this section on "What Causes Love" are designed to thoroughly familiarize you with these key aspects of personality in others. They will give you the background necessary to identify them insightfully when that is what's going to count the most. Then the subsequent parts of the book will show you how to go about putting these new insights to work.

The most important thing needed by anyone who wants to spark someone else's passion is having a realistic outlook in their understanding of love. Only by knowing what produces this emotion in others is it possible to deliberately make it happen. Accordingly, as you go through the first section there may be moments when you will feel more like a student of psychology than a student of seduction. Frankly, a small fraction of what this section contains is deep. But the fact is that love is nothing if not deep. So go ahead and delve, get immersed, for it will pay deep dividends soon enough.

Now let's direct our attention at the basics. As we review these, your insight will become deeper. And that will sharpen the most important tool pertinent to affairs of the heart. This involves the cooperation, the linking, of your heart with your mind. The fact is that nothing can point out our goals better than our hearts, while nothing will ensure our attaining them better than actively employing our minds.

CHAPTER TWO

WHAT THE OTHER PERSON EXPERIENCES WHEN THEY ARE IN LOVE

Before going further, bear in mind that our primary aim is to see what goes on in the OTHER person's mind. Obviously, everything we've said up to now also applies to you. When you get involved with someone, you are going to feel more or less as they do, that is, your sense of identity is bound to be affected too. However, in this book we are going to stay clear of the issues surrounding the other person's impact on you.

Most other books about love and romance only focus on the demands a relationship places on its reader. For the most part they dwell on your hangups and ways to overcome these. But while the perspective of these other books may instill a measure of hope, there's still the practical question of what you can do to win another person's love.

Naturally you possess certain needs and preferences, and if they are not met in a given relationship, that might jeopardize the whole thing. But that is a topic for a different book. Here our overriding concern will be exclusively with SEDUCTION: the issue of getting *another* person to fall deeply and permanently in love with you.

How-to books that try to help you solve your own personality problems may give some people the hope they need to start searching for love. But merely venturing out, brimming with hope, seldom works as well as the factually-based method this book is going to give you. Through our approach you will become adept at relating to the facets of another's identity which predispose *them* to fall in love; once you're familiar with the best way to do this you can apply it in a genuinely seductive manner, first to win and then to keep the kind of relationship we all hope for.

* * *

To fully understand what makes a person fall in love, let's begin by looking at how someone who is in love would experience this state, that is, how they would be affected by it. Why? Because the more conscious you become of the condition you want to create, the easier it will be to go about doing it.

So let's start by separating the part of the experience associated with receiving love from the part operating when a person is giving it. There are two poles to this experience. First, there is what someone experiences in their own mind when they feel loved. Then there is how they express their love toward someone else. We must look at these things separately if we wish to understand either one clearly.

Of course both parts represent aspects of the same experience. But it is the part a person experiences *when they feel that they are being loved* that can teach us the most. From a *tactical* perspective, this will show us some very important things about what it takes to make someone feel this way.

A SENSE OF SELF-WORTH

When someone feels loved, the main thing they experience is a warm, pleasant sensation of well-being and self-satisfaction. Naturally, this good feeling doesn't just happen. It happens in response to someone else's attitude. Now let's say you are this other person; in that case the significance of your attitude would lie in the reinforcement it lends to your partner's good feelings. Normally just your attitude is enough to produce a state of well-being in the other. A lover *gives* the one who feels loved a concrete reason to feel self-satisfied.

With few exceptions, the good feeling comes about because the one who feels loved recognizes that you put great stock in their personal worth. As one philosopher described being on the receiving end: "I find that I count for something to the other."[1] Nothing is as central to the question of love as the *validation* of someone's worth. Taken together, love is a show of admiration on one side, and the sense of worth that is experienced on the other. When your partner feels loved they experience the reality of their worth through your independent viewpoint.

It isn't simply that a lover validates the other's value. But since this does happen, it can seem that what's involved here is just a question of someone getting their ego stroked. However, the issue involves much more than someone stepping into a spotlight to enjoy applause.

As modern man became less group-oriented and more individualized, everyone's need for tangible demonstrations of approval from others has grown stronger than ever. Irrespective of the telephone company, today we're all more disconnected than was formerly the case. In the traditional group setting of past ages, most people remained fairly self-satisfied merely through being accepted members of a tightly-knit group. In a sense, the group itself was a sort of collective psychic sanctuary for each member's sense of worth. As long as people did nothing to risk their "reputation," (which meant acting out a set role within the group) they enjoyed an easy acceptance on the psychological plane. A healthy sense of self-worth used to prevail as a matter of course.

Today, however, the group's significance has declined. The sense of belonging and acceptability that most people felt within groups has pretty much disappeared. Now to maintain a sense of personal worth each of us needs someone else's discernable acts of validation. Rather than being an automatic result of group solidarity, a sense of personal worth has to be sought independently by each person on their own.

But as you know, modern existence offers us few opportunities to experience our worth simply in terms of who we are. All of us are involved in situations where our personal value is estimated on the basis of society's 9 to 5 measures of success. Yet even when those paths to a sense of worth are open to us, they are generally associated with aspects of ourselves which are secondary, and not the most important. By contrast, when someone feels loved, this touches directly on the most movingly personal aspects of their self-identity.

This is why love is no longer merely an exciting pastime for princes and princesses, as it was some centuries ago. With the decline of traditional bonds, and our current absorption in our own independent identity, a need of equal proportions has arisen among all of us for the approval of others. In fact we have a heightened preoccupation with "reputation" and "prestige," because these are no longer automatically given to us simply because of our membership in a group.

Therefore when someone finds that they "count for something to the other," this provides them a kind of approval which is equal to what was previously obtained in groups. Now it is mostly in the private position of a personal relationship that people get to register a sense of their "true" worth. This is what makes love an indispensable part of modern existence, rather than merely an ego trip.

A FEELING OF JOY

The next thing to recognize is that love is a subjective feeling, that is, a feeling we have within ourselves on our own terms. Though people will attribute this feeling to admirable qualities in their partner, the major source of how they feel has a purely internal reference point. When someone is in love, the way they feel results from the enhancing effect that *you* have on the way *they feel about themselves*. What they experience in their own mind is passive, not active. It is based on their receiving your affection, not on their reasoned judgments about you. The feeling mainly reflects their *acceptance* of your positive thoughts about them.

The way you relate to someone can have consequences bearing on their most intimate feelings about themselves. When this is negative or derogatory, everyone responds with an actively defensive reaction. But when it's positive the only effort they expend is in making sure that it gets fully savored.

If it sounds strange to hear that love has a passive side to it, that's because we generally don't focus on just the receiving end. But no one feels "in love" until they have taken in another's impression and been profoundly affected by it. It is the assimilation of another's positive impression that creates the feeling. In a way the feeling builds the same way a plant passively absorbs moisture from the air.

Still, if we were to ask anyone who is in love how this came about, they would place most of the emphasis on the fact that they admire something about their partner. This is to be expected, given the main focus of their attention. Normally people are more consciously absorbed with their partner's significance than with the feeling they are experiencing within their own mind.

Nevertheless, when someone feels loved it is because they have already concluded that your admiration is inspired by the qualities which you find in them. Several specific things in the way you respond unmistakably conveys that you view them positively. There don't have to be any major compliments on your part for this sense of approval to be felt. Their expectation that approval can occur, and their hope that it will, makes them feel that it has. They become persuaded that you only see their better qualities. This is one of those times in life when it is enough to experience something without questioning every detail. The other person finds that for a penetrating moment a feeling can mean exactly what they take it to mean.

A person's mind can accent almost anything that happens. Then what is focused upon becomes dominant and makes everything else conform to it. The individual is worked up into a state in which they feel valued in terms of the person they happen to be. Having experienced the uncertainty of a relationship which in one sense can be viewed as a weighing of their attractiveness, or acceptability, each sign of approval touches the core of their wish to *feel* as valuable as possible.

Contrary to Dale Carnegie's suggestion that people merely want to *look* important or seem valuable, people actually want to *feel* valuable, to have significance, to be worthy. The other person's basic impulse is not merely to seem to be all of these things in your eyes, but *actually to feel* that they are this way. Gradually, as they can interpret your response as supporting just this feeling in them, and without words of love or romance themselves having been spoken, that person will feel loved.

A COMBINED SENTIMENT OF WHOLENESS

Another characteristic of feeling loved is the heightened sense of themselves that a person gets from this experience. There is an expansion of their self-awareness which includes several aspects of their identity, aspects that lie closest to their heart, so to speak. Soon they come to feel as if these aspects are all harmoniously fused. They find themselves enjoying a sense of *wholeness* that had gone unfelt for too long. As the philosopher Nietzsche put it, "One seems to oneself transfigured, stronger, richer, more complete: one is more complete."

In essence, this sense of completion comes from their being appreciated in the same way in which they fundamentally conceptualize themselves, that is, in terms of their own self-image. And given what everyone's personality is made up of, this image always contains three basic things.

To be more specific, love grows out of a combination of factors that are fundamental parts of everyone's self-identity. These include, first, the individual's "sense of gender," secondly, the sense of belonging with others, that is, the "social self," and third, a sense of their own potential ability, or as this is usually referred to, the "ideal self-image."

The *combined reaction* generated by these three components of personality creates the emotional base out of which the experience of love arises. These three aspects of our self-image generate love because each of us experiences our most personally-felt sense of worth with respect to all three of them.

UNCONDITIONAL WORTH AND LOVE

By this point you may be wondering why these three particular aspects of identity are the only ones directly implicated with love. Why not something else, like the part of our self-image that applies to one's intelligence? The reason is that in order for anyone to experience love, they have to be affected *on the most fundamental level on which they identify themselves.* And it so happens that this deeply authentic level of personality is made up *exclusively* by the three core aspects that we are concentrating on. Human nature being what it is, these three aspects are the only intrinsically unconditional parts of our identity.

28

Most other aspects of our personality reflect roles that are conditional; they are roles in which we act out conventional routines. Therefore a sense of unconditional worth can only come from the three core aspects of identity that are most deeply woven into a person's being. That is the only level where a person can experience a sense of their *unconditional* worth.

What makes the act of loving someone so unique is that it allows them to get in touch with their own more or less unconditional sense of inherent worth. This prospect is present because when the situation a person gets into has romantic possibilities, their physical needs puts the focus on their gender identity; their need for a sense of belonging puts the focus on their social self-image; and their desire to be considered special focuses on their self-ideal and casts it in the leading role.

Now these three aspects of identity are the main source of a person's sense of unconditional worth. These alone form the core of the most authentically personal side of a person, the basis of what they know they are essentially and unconditionally. So these aspects of identity alone serve as the source for this rare and special feeling.

* * *

Another thing that has to be emphasized is that each of these three components of identity is responsible for a specific "feeling of self." The gender specific, social, and ideal aspects of our identities have a felt quality which is experienced subjectively inside ourselves. These inner feelings reflect the degree of satisfaction or dissatisfaction associated with what each of us thinks about ourselves.

William James was the first to refer to this subjective side of our experience as "self-feelings." As James put this:

> . . . there is a certain average tone of self-feeling which each one of us carries about with him, and which is independent of the objective reasons we may have for satisfaction or discontent . . . These are primarily *self-* and *self-dissatisfaction* . . . Language has synonyms enough for both primary feelings. Thus pride, conceit, vanity, self-esteem, arrogance, vainglory, on the one hand; and on the other modesty, humility, confusion, shame, and personal despair. These two opposite classes of affection seem to be direct and elementary endowments of our nature . . . like rage or pain.[2]

This accounts for the distinctly *emotional* quality that is experienced in a love relation. The interior emotional state a person experiences when they are in love comes from *a combined feeling of self-satisfaction encompassing the sexual, social and ideal aspects of their identity*.

Once you fully appreciate that all these aspects of your partner's personality must be addressed in order to evoke passion, you will be prepared to win the only kind of love worth seducing someone for. When anyone gets positive responses with regard to these aspects of their self-image, they will feel the pleasure that comes when the way you view them is in harmony with how they would most want to be seen. If they feel that it is actually the best they can be that has been duly recognized and fully appreciated, they will soon feel that they are loved and in love.

* * *

Before we explore these facets of identity more closely, let's see why they can give rise to such a profound reaction. In order to understand love, it has to be taken apart to see its basic ingredients. However, real life experience doesn't reveal this division. Love is felt as a single all inclusive reality which totally envelops one's being. So let's take an even wider perspective, one that includes both the "what" and the "why."

CHAPTER THREE

LOVE IS A WAY TO EXPERIENCE A FORM OF COMPLETE FULFILLMENT

The most basic thing about love is that it always touches on issues which involve the outcome of three deeply personal concerns. "Does he appreciate the woman that I am?" "Does she think I can handle things; does she feel secure with me? "Does he enjoy just being alone with me; is he going to stay with me permanently?" "Does she feel that we belong together, that we are meant for each other?" "Does he appreciate the significance of my goals?" "Does she sense my latent possibilities, what I am capable of, if I were given a chance?"

What makes questions like these crucial in generating love is that they all represent something that has a bearing on a person's sense of identity. But in order to fully appreciate why these aspects of identity play such a pivotal role in love we also have to see what's ultimately at stake in this context.

To begin with, what counts in a loving relationship involves our appreciation of who someone really is in themselves; all outward considerations become secondary. Neither their diplomas, their inheritances, nor even their knowledge, are the values which matter in this situation. Everyone wants an authentically romantic response in terms of who they really are fundamentally. Now, if we look more closely at what lies behind this, we'll find what's truly at stake.

Beneath the mental level on which this response is being consciously pursued *every living human being has a permanent indwelling wish to be fulfilled.* Though seldom spoken of, or focused on at length, this desire has a definite place in everybody's mind. And when love becomes a likely prospect, it is fully awakened. A wish for fulfillment is what anyone on love's doorstep is ultimately seeking to gratify.

In our society this very normal thirst for fulfillment is more commonly associated with attaining a high status, or with acquiring certain fabulous objects. But even when expressed with regard to these widely sought aims, what's actually at the base of our longing for fulfillment concerns the impression our possession of those things would make on others. In other words, the objects or status we dream about are but conspicuous outward symbols that would confirm the worth that already exists within all of us. Such things would merely prove our worth to others.

In short, regardless of what form it takes, the human longing for fulfillment is always related to our own innermost sense of personal value.

This bears repeating: whichever way a person may envision their own complete fulfillment, this ultimately represents what such fulfillment would say about who she or he really is. The hifalutin ways we ordinarily picture what it would take for us to be totally fulfilled, be it in terms of wealth or celebrity, is no more than an image our mind creates when we ponder how we might get to be all that we deserve to be. Our sense of self is both the plot and star in the mental drama we build around our notions of fulfillment.

And yet, most of our everyday routines only provide us superficial fulfillments. We are obliged to spend a good deal of time putting forward only a small portion of our identities in impersonal contexts. Even if we play a leading role, the most meaningful aspects of our identities are seldom brought into play.

By contrast, during the emotional interaction of a man and a woman the most meaningful aspects of our identities are continuously being revealed. This creates a context in which we can feel that virtually the whole of our self is being fulfilled. And because a romantic relation always involves several basic aspects of our personality almost simultaneously, fulfillment is not only conceivable, *but attainable.*

In love the intended and achieved union of a man and woman generates a level of satisfaction that is experienced globally. This global significance grows out of what objectively appears like only a small area of give and take. Yet to those experiencing it within their own mind, the encounter represents a situation in which one can pour out their whole soul amid the incomparable authenticity evoked by the other's presence.

This places us in a state of harmony with the sexual, social, and hope-oriented aspects of our personalities. So what each person finds goes beyond being just an incomparable joy or a continuing contentment and becomes a combination of both. Love *is* a mode of complete fulfillment.

* * *

The point is this: the phenomenon of love, what it is, and "why" it has to be what it is, is in the end traceable to a person's inherent capacity to experience a state of total fulfillment. Since certain episodes in a relationship involve the satisfaction of a person's deepest self-feelings, eventually these repeated satisfactions have a cumulative effect which consummates anyone's capacity to feel fulfilled: each part contributes to the total feeling, and the total feeling contributes to the intensity felt in each part — till one's limit is reached.

This also happens because it isn't in the nature of the urge for fulfillment to just sit there waiting indefinitely for some future success. However much life may appear bent on postponing its realization, certain unmistakable joys can take on a significance which bridges the distinction between partial and complete self-enjoyment. With certain ends that are reachable, once we lay hold of them — there is little more left to want. Orgasms sometimes feel like that, but sensing the immediacy of one's own unconditional worth *always* feels like this.

As a motive for behavior, the wish to be fulfilled tends to color any situation where it seems attainable. Since everyone has a built-in capacity to *be* fulfilled, to the extent that this is lacking, it sets up an urge to find it. Love is what a person seeking fulfillment wants it to be: love, the loved one finds, is that who they are as a person is considered worthwhile, and this is enough to make them feel completely fulfilled.

Love is being known as the person you are and admired for it. In a process unique to humans, we see the very essence of another person's essential nature, with all the virtues they possess. Even though some of these virtues may remain hidden, the influence that love has on our perception allows us to appreciate the reality of someone's ultimate worth. And by being seen in this light, they in turn feel that their deepest longing to have their worth known has been realized.

In the final analysis the existence of love is based on our inborn capacity to enjoy this world and to derive our share of the fulfillment all of us are entitled to. Each person can realize his or her hope of experiencing a state of complete fulfillment simply because they are who they happen to be. Civilized life has a "rule book" of civilized conditions for getting to this simple birth right, but a deep wave of passion casts aside conditions, and what was simply given is simply realized. It is hard to find anything more fulfilling than this.

* * *

Yes, the stakes will be high in any seduction. After all, love is not a zero-sum game where one person's gain can be won at another's expense. In love both win or no one does. However, in order to ensure that you fully receive what can only be gotten from another, you should do whatever you can to refine the skill needed to secure this.

Since love is based on a person's deepest longing for fulfillment, providing something of this magnitude may seem like quite an enormous proposition. However when someone starts to fall in love with you, it will be because they have come to feel that you are capable of satisfying at least some aspects of that longing. In time, if they continue to experience your willingness, they will begin to feel that there is reason to hope that the full scope of their longings will be granted too.

But before another person's feelings lead them to expect this kind of fulfillment, seduction assumes your readiness to address the needs, wishes, desires, hopes, and requests which underlie that person's deepest longings. Responding to all of this does stand to be quite a tall order, unless you genuinely understand which of these demands are really crucial.

Generally only the last of the various demands mentioned above, the requests, will be expressed, in so many words, by the other. The rest remain unspoken and have to be inferred within the varying contexts of a relationship. Normally our ability to empathize with others allows us to identify the unspoken hopes that someone else brings to our encounters. The details you are about to examine next are going to increase the effectiveness of your ability to do this through an empowering foreknowledge.

Shortly your capacity to discern another's longings will become thoroughly seductive. When any factor which can trigger feelings of love in your partner makes its appearance, you will be fully alert to the ones that count most. And by familiarizing yourself with the three paramount needs which lead others to feel love, this foreknowledge will give you ample reason to be confident that when the occasion arises, you will get precisely what you want.

* * *

To summarize: when William James wrote, "The deepest principle in human nature is the craving to be appreciated," he wasn't thinking about love, but he could just as well have been.

CHAPTER FOUR

THE ROOTS OF LOVE

When someone is falling in love they experience an all encompassing feeling which makes them unaware that three distinct parts of their personality are being satisfied. Yes, it's possible for them to be attracted or to get infatuated with you even when you've only related to a single aspect of their personality. But the prospect of their being completely aroused won't fully materialize until you have an effect that touches on their sense of unconditional worth. To do this you have to address the three facets of their identity which are most deeply rooted in the core of their being.

Stated briefly, romantic love is an inward feeling in which the sexual, social, and ideal aspects of a person's identity have all been gratified one after the other. After your partner has hung in there despite alternating hopes and doubts during successive encounters, each of these aspects of their identity has to wind up receiving just the response they needed.

So before we get to the nuts and bolts of our strategy, let's take a closer in-depth look at these three factors. As we already said, seduction hinges on your familiarity with each of love's ingredients. To respond appropriately to these specific aspects of another's identity, a seducer must be thoroughly acquainted with each one. Once you have completed this chapter, we will be in a good position to discuss the best way to gratify someone in a way they've always dreamed of.

GENDER IDENTITY AND LOVE*

From the start, a romantic relationship has the aura of being something fated. Once an interest has been indicated on both sides, the other person will feel as if they were being moved by a process with its own momentum. They will have a sense that what is taking place fits in with some deeper purpose.

As we saw in the last chapter, this mood stems from a hazy suspicion that their personal value is about to be appreciated. And at the beginning their sense of gender identity has a major impact on creating this mood. This results from the context created when a man and a woman first draw together in a private interaction. Any spark of interest tends to have an immediate heterosexual flavor, because this is the most prominent thing initially defining a couple's combined presence. For each person this becomes a feelable, knowable measure of how well they are being received by the other.

Most people are thoroughly conditioned to act in a way that is in line with their society's definition of gender roles. There exist distinctive roles for each sex, as well as standard ways to act these out. Accordingly, members of each sex have a powerful

---

* The following discussion refers to heterosexuals only. Homosexual relations and the role that gender identity plays in them require a separate discussion which is not undertaken here. However, subsequent sections are pertinent to everyone.

unconscious drive to exhibit the attributes that are supposed to characterize their own sex. This includes some reference to one's body, but it mainly involves certain features of one's personal conduct. Psychologists refer to this latter issue as a person's sense of their "sexual identity."

But few people of either sex always feel sure that they completely live up to the conventionally glorified standards of their respective gender roles. Most of us tend to think that some special ability is required to act out these stereotypes. Your new friend is therefore likely to have a built-in drive to find support and approval for this aspect of their identity.

Since this aspect of the other's identity is not just a question of their physical being, but simultaneously involves how they act out a particular gender role, a question can always arise as to how well that person performs this role. This is particularly so with respect to certain aspects of their sexual identity which mainly have a functional significance for members of the opposite sex. Such things as a male's virility, or a woman's sensuous appeal, can really only be confirmed through an appropriate response from someone of the other sex.

The start of a potentially romantic interaction always brings this issue forward (even though it generally remains beneath the surface). Because certain aspects of everyone's sexual identity need to be confirmed by a member of the opposite sex, they are disposed to a strong emotional reaction whenever they do receive an approving response. When he is playing masculine or she is playing feminine and you appear a bit turned on, they feel this impacting directly on this facet of themselves.

In part, of course, this situation generally stimulates a trace of erotic arousal. But what prompts this arousal is seldom simply physical. As one of the leading authorities on the psychology of sex, Dr. Albert Ellis has noted, "Sex arousal . . . is only partly mediated through nerve pathways that are set in motion through physical or bodily stimulation. It is most importantly, in addition, the result of brain processes: of thinking and emoting . . . *the head and the heart* rather than the lips, fingers, arms, and genitals are the main organs of arousing and satisfying one's mate."[1] (my italics)

This is why, when real love is someone's goal, their sexual urges are filtered through an essentially personal side of their psyche, more specifically, the one connected to their gender identity. Moreover, because it gets blended with an identity need, sex acquires a wider ranging significance. Rather than just being physically stimulated, the other will feel a deeply personal involvement which is thoroughly engrossing. In the presence of someone who is personally meaningful, they will feel a vague need that was looking for a way to express itself. Her sense of femaleness or his sense of maleness will clearly register the opportunity for a real confirmation.

So to begin with, keep in mind that when you first encounter someone in a potentially romantic context they will probably make some show of gender, often without consciously intending to. When this happens, they will be seeking not only your confirmation of its appropriateness, but above all else — how agreeable you find it.

We will deal with this topic again from a completely tactical standpoint in Chapter Thirteen. For now remember that everyone attaches a deeply personal importance to finding someone whose response will enhance the sexual aspect of their identity; moreover, this will be the case even though they may not be particularly conscious of needing this kind of confirmation. But when this confirmation *is* forthcoming, it will produce a definite attraction to the one who provides it.

THE SOCIAL SELF: BELONGING WITH SOMEONE

Offhand it's not always apparent that the purely social side of our nature plays a powerful role in our love relations. Ordinarily it seems as if love is a separate thing unto itself. And yet, while there is certainly good reason to separate social from romantic contexts, as a rule the underlying social impulse has a way of filtering into our private intimate relations too.

The reason this happens lies in our mind's completely normal habit of diverting impulses that haven't been fully gratified into areas where gratification can be found. Since most people pass much of their time in highly impersonal interactions, when they get close to us romantically we take on an added significance. Not only do we act as a focal point for their romantic longings, but we also serve as an outlet for those aspects of their social nature which go unmet in today's impersonal society.

Actually, love hasn't always functioned as an outlet for the social impulse the way it does today.

Not long ago this form of "sublimation" served a different impulse the same way. In fact, love's ability to function as an outlet for other unmet needs was discovered in connection with sex.

Sigmund Freud was the first to see that much of love's driving force comes from something besides our openly romantic sentiments. He found that unfulfilled sexual desires regularly worked their way into romantic relations in an indirect way. This was fairly common during the Victorian period. Freud therefore concluded that the intensity of romantic feelings is produced by more than just those motives found on the surface.

There is little doubt that he was basically right about this; any impulse which is routinely kept from being fulfilled tends to become stronger and to seek the handiest available outlet. However, for that to happen, the impulse in question would have to be under continuous restraint. Generally this sort of continuous inhibition results from the currently accepted standards in a given society. Such inhibiting standards did exist with respect to sex in the Viennese society of Freud's day.

But while that form of sexual channeling was no doubt common during the Victorian period, today things are quite different. As Rollo May recently observed, the changes wrought by the sexual revolution have made people in our society far less restrained about sex than they are about engaging in person-to-person intimacy.[2]

This was vividly brought home to me several years ago when a friend, then in his late twenties, who after just having described a fantastic night of sex with a woman he had only recently met was asked if he planned to take her to an upcoming party. "No way!" he replied with real alarm, "I don't know how we'd get along. We only know each other physically."

Another example which illustrates that "getting along" is often more problematical than sex comes from one of my former clients. He was a man in his mid-thirties who, despite more than a decade of active dating and an ample number of sexual encounters, was deeply depressed about his failure to find a woman he considered "marriage material." The lack of lasting love in his life had resulted in a diminishing level of energy when it came to his continuing the pursuit of the kind of love he actually wanted.

This man was well-versed in sexual lore, and confided to me that he owned and had read a large number of works on sexual techniques and practices. When I asked whether he had ever studied other disciplines, like social-psychology, communications and listening, or any other subject that might contribute to his ability to handle himself well in the sort of loving relationship he had unsuccessfully sought, he expressed some surprise that any such topics should be a focus in his case. But then he admitted that he had never seriously studied or worked on any of these areas with anything like the zeal he had devoted to "how-to" sex manuals.

With further counseling this man came to realize that he had never worked at really listening to, or at genuinely understanding any of the women with whom he had had his quickly consummated, quickly-ended, non-intimate yet sexual relationships. His situation changed as he gradually came to understand that his expertise as a sexual technician did little to prepare him to meet another person's need for purely social relatedness. Once he genuinely accepted that his love life would never be what the manuals promised until he made knowing a woman on a personally intimate basis as important as he had made knowing her physically, his romantic fortunes changed dramatically. Two months after he learned the basic realities of interpersonal accommodation (described in Part Five of this book) and did the spadework that allowed him to effectively put his insight into practice, he entered a relationship which promises to remain everything he and *she* always really wanted.

* * *

The sexual revolution has made the sex act more permissible, but has done little to help show people how to reach the social level of intimacy from which sexual relations follow as an irresistible and natural outcome. Frankly, anyone seeking real love in today's world has to focus on what is currently much more likely to be needed by others. The fact is that while there is definitely still an impulse from another part of the psyche feeding romantic feelings, this added need now comes mainly from the social side of our nature.

Other people have to be responded to in a certain way in order for them to get the sense of belonging they require to sustain their own social self-image. Everyone's inborn social nature involves a need to be in possession of a sense of belonging or inclusion with others. But in our society this recognition and acceptance often winds up being accessible to most people only in a private, personal situation.

This is a very recent addition to mating patterns. It came about from the loosening of communal relations which has occurred during the past century. A few generations ago people were able to gratify their social impulses fairly easily, in town squares, public gathering places, and among members of their extended families.[3] But today, many of our natural social needs have been left stranded. And when these needs are not met, they don't simply evaporate, as anyone who has felt the pangs of real loneliness already knows.

After all, our built-in social impulses haven't been bred out of us yet. Consequently, because it's so hard to find existing communal areas in which these impulses can be fully gratified, they get funneled into the only area left for such gratification. What has changed is not the nature or strength of the social impulse but the increasingly impersonal nature of society, and so the situations left in which to truly satisfy this impulse.

Because lovers don't just relate to each other on the surface, this permits them to get totally involved with every aspect of themselves. This includes their social impulse, which reacts to the interpersonal context by seeking the quality and intensity of interpersonal involvement that is needed to experience a sense of belonging.

Furthermore, the satisfaction two people receive privately in terms of their social identity isn't any less meaningful than what was previously obtained in groups. It's a special sense of solidarity, different in that it applies to just you and them. But though it lacks the hoopla associated with larger groups, it produces the same sense of inclusion. Without oaths, or banners, just the two of you know you belong.

* * *

Because of the depth of feeling associated with the need for a sense of belonging, one of the most important requirements for creating love involves the degree of "interpersonal rapport" that is generated by two particular people. When a man and a woman can accommodate or go along with one another's way of relating on purely interpersonal terms, they begin to feel that they *belong* with each other.

What this "accommodating" comes down to involves how a person's usual way of relating fares with a particular partner. This determines how much personal rapport they experience. Later, when I describe the strategy required to respond to this component of love, you will find that another's social identity is expressed in one of two ways. There are two distinct ways in which people characteristically relate to others, that of the extrovert, and that of the introvert. Evoking genuine emotional rapport involves responding appropriately to this part of a person's individual make-up.

For now it is enough if you recognize that love feeds heavily from a person's need to attain a sense of belonging with you. Love must allow room for the sense of belonging which is so difficult to find anywhere else. When you are alone together with someone, this will afford their social identity one of its few sources of genuine validation. And by providing this you will show them that love is not only doubly involving, but that it can be doubly delicious.

THE SELF-IDEAL

Anyone who experiences a confirmation and acceptance of the two identity needs we have covered so far would no doubt feel deeply gratified. And yet in order for them to fall passionately in love something more would still be needed. Love derives its full impetus from three sources. And each one has to contribute its share.

True passion, and its accompanying ecstasy, is something rare because love's third ingredient doesn't always get its due. This component of love is commonly referred to as a person's *self-ideal*; it involves that part of their self-identity which represents the best that they feel capable of being.

Looked at closely, this facet of someone's self-image is built up around their inner reserves of unenacted potential. A person's hidden capacities influence them to make general assumptions about what they may be capable of. In turn these assumptions become a specific part of their self-identity, which is symbolized as the "self-ideal." (See Section III of the Appendix for a full explanation).

The ideal aspect of personality holds a significant position for an overwhelming majority of people. No one forms a final image of themselves merely on the basis of the limits which may be imposed by their existing circumstances. As long as they remain mentally sound, they keep a sense of what they might be able to do under favorable conditions.[4] And this is not just a fleeting hope that comes and goes, but constitutes a permanent part of each person's sense of self. But even more important, this particular aspect of identity is responsible for the most intense and personal feeling which leads a given person to fall in love.

* * *

What will ultimately induce love in another person is for you to perceive them in a way that acknowledges the value *they* feel they possess, *even when they haven't actually displayed this openly.*

As a rule, a person's estimate of themselves includes certain capacities they know they possess, but which may not have gained any outward recognition in their world yet. Nevertheless these self-estimates do reflect an accurate reading of that person's latent potential. So when you allow room — even indirectly — for its existence, this will strike a very responsive chord in them.

Stated differently, the third component of love involves a person's latent capacities, those which may not yet have attained any outwardly acknowledged status. Nevertheless, in a lover's eyes, someone who everyone else views as ordinary or average stands out as the most perfect being in the world. Apparently a lover sees something the others don't. Probably the others haven't bothered to look deeply enough into that person.

What anyone will consider a truly romantic attitude on your part involves your having an exceptionally high estimation of them. A "beloved" holds an exalted position because you apparently recognize attributes in them which merit high approval. Indirectly, this leads them to believe that they have been singled out because of the higher accomplishment that they may be capable of. Your estimation serves to confirm the other's self-ideal.

* * *

Before a person meets the one they will fall in love with, a deep desire born out of their self-feelings make them ready for this to happen. The most powerful of these feelings is an inner tension between what that individual believes him or herself capable of being, and how little of that they have been able to work into their lives up to the present moment.

To a certain degree, people are preoccupied with being something greater than others presently perceive them as being. They are still asking the eternal questions: What am I? What is my destiny? With a lover's acceptance, the beloved feels that such questions are resolved by that acceptance. A lover's perception always recognizes certain ideal qualities in a beloved which ordinarily go unnoticed.

Ordinarily the hidden potential which underlies a person's self-ideal is weighed by most people only in terms of what such a person has concretely accomplished. However, a lover weighs the beloved's personal capacities not in terms of recorded facts, but on the level of their potential value within their own lives. A lover confirms the value of another's hidden resources, despite the crowd's indifference.

Through the validation and confirmation that a person's self-ideal receives in a relationship, their unrealized potential is transformed from its lesser, to its more positive significance. But it takes your presence for them to feel this way. Then perhaps they will admit, as Roy Croft did, that "I love you not only for what you are, but for what I am when I am with you . . ."

PART II

A STRATEGY OF SEDUCTION

Every minute now
Should be the father of some stratagem.

SHAKESPEARE,
HENRY IV, Part 2

She must owe me nothing, for she must be free; love exists only in freedom, only in freedom is there enjoyment and everlasting delight. Although I am aiming at her falling into my arms as it were by a natural necessity, yet I am striving to bring it about so that as she gravitates toward me, it will . . . be like . . . spirit seeking spirit . . . Practically, I have reached the point where I desire nothing which is not, in the strictest sense, freely given.

SOREN KIERKEGAARD,
Diary of the Seducer

CHAPTER FIVE

THE TECHNIQUE OF SEDUCTION

H aving another person's love is one of the few things that can bring practically anyone a real sense of fulfillment. And yet many people who haven't got this never try to find out how they might go about getting it. The reason these people don't bother is that they've accepted the myth that love is something mysterious. Since anything considered mysterious is by implication also uncontrollable, they leave their romantic hopes completely up to fate. But then when a new relationship isn't going the way they hoped, or an existing one starts to fall apart, they also end up having to resign themselves to "the inevitable."

Actually, though, as we just saw, love is not as mysterious as most of its advocates would have us believe. After completing the chapters in the first part of this book, you now have a fairly thorough command of the three factors which must be addressed to evoke virtually anyone's more impassioned response. Now that you've seen what actually leads people to fall in love, you are in a position to decisively influence your romantic fortunes whenever and with whoever you are inspired to.

To consolidate your deepened insight into these matters let us shift gears now. To draw up a strategy of seduction we need to convert the facts we've considered into an approach that can produce tangible results. This means that we must concentrate on the underlying motives within your partner which, as we have seen, are what give rise to love.

* * *

Speaking generally, the foundation of our strategy is based on conveying three specific kinds of affirmation. First you have to show your delight in the other's attractiveness as a man or a woman. This will get them interested in you in a way which has definite erotic implications.

Secondly, your response to them should be as congenial as possible to their particular way of relating, so as to create the kind of rapport that says you belong together. And thirdly, you must express your recognition of everything that you consider extraordinary about them, so as to validate the legitimacy of the ideal side of their identity.

Looked at on its broadest terms, seduction involves your conveying a subtle yet distinct impression of what you think the person you've chosen is like. The surest way to connect romantically with someone is to show them that you are pleased with the kind of person they are; the kind of man or woman they are, the kind of companion they make, and how promising their future seems to you considering what they are capable of, which you accept as being a deeper characteristic of that person.

You can't show that you're pleased with all these things in one sitting. Still, once there's been time for each to be acknowledged your partner will want nothing as much as to prove that you were right in being pleased.

But keep in mind that it's not so much what each of these aspects of their identity represent in themselves. Their potential impact lies in the significance they have taken together. What makes them a key to love is their susceptibility to forging an exclusive emotional link to someone who values all of them. Deriving gratification from one source is the solvent that will bind their heart to yours.

What will take place resembles the workings of a high-tech pinball machine; once you've touched on these three aspects seductively, all the high-scoring lights will go on. And once they are all on, each time a ball touches a terminal the score will multiply explosively until you've won the game.

* * *

Less metaphorically, a person will be drawn to fall in love with you through the pleasurable feelings which you produce in them. However this feeling won't come about by showing them how much you need them. If anything, your neediness says more about you than about them. Strictly speaking, seduction involves projecting your appreciation of whatever makes them desirable, and not how much you may want or need such things yourself.

Seduction is a matter of being impressed just enough with someone's finer qualities for them to know that these show. But this has to be just so, because you don't want to gloat over a quality so much that it appears as if you're in need of such a quality yourself.

Subsequent chapters will describe this overall approach in much greater detail. However outside the covers of this book your relationship will be a unique situation, with its own rhythm of integration and rate of development. Therefore it will be best if we first consider the underlying premise on which our strategy is based.

EMOTIONAL PREDISPOSITIONS AND SEDUCTION

Let's start by seeing why an approach based on foreknowledge can safely replace the old reliance on luck, lipstick, tight jeans and other time worn mediums of ingratiation. Actually, and of far greater consequence for seduction, anyone about to fall in love is always unconsciously striving to gratify certain specific aspects of their personality. Rather than involving everything about a person, it is only those needs which are directly tied to an individual's sense of worth that ultimately end up generating romantic feelings in them. Viewed tactically, what you need to focus on is the fact that there are only three basic needs which have this kind of intrinsically romantic implication.

As a rule most people don't look at love this objectively. Consequently they don't take into account the needs in themselves, or in their partner, that are actually pressing for satisfaction. They simply view love as something that occurs entirely in response to individuals who possess certain visibly appealing characteristics. But because of this, when these people dwell on what is required to make someone else love them, they stay stuck on the same old issue — they are mainly concerned about their own exterior qualities.

Now if this naive perspective were the whole story there wouldn't be very much to say about seduction, except to recommend ways of sprucing up our outward appearance. In fact though, beyond this oversimplified consideration, what your future partner will be unconsciously predisposed for will be to having certain very specific personal wishes gratified.

Even if someone gets caught up in assessing your observable exterior credentials, their subjective longing for personal fulfillment predisposes them to react automatically when you touch certain crucial response chords. And this predisposition is always there regardless of what they may be consciously caught up on.

The fact is that the major part of this process comes about less consciously than most people realize. No one arrives at his or her feelings of love while they are weighing things that they can assess consciously. This is why two strangers usually find it hard to explain the feeling of connectedness they often experience right away. As Stendahl, an early student of this phenomenon observed:

> Love is like (a) fever, it is born and spends itself without the slightest intervention of the (conscious) will . . . Man is not free to avoid doing that which gives him more pleasure to do than all other possible actions.[1]

Of course no one ever actually falls in love without some sense of what's happening. Taken together another person's romantic interest always involves a combination of two factors: first there is how that person perceives you, and secondly, how they are *subjectively affected by you*. But of these two processes the latter one is far and away of much greater consequence.

For the sake of emphasis let's say someone's outward perception doesn't lead them to make a favorable judgement about you right away. Nevertheless, the part that usually goes without notice, which involves how they are affected subjectively, can lead them to a favorable judgement irrespective of anything else. Every time you see a couple where one is noticeably more outwardly attractive than the other, it is a living example of this. Actually it's little wonder because love is a spontaneous process which grips people mainly on an unconscious plane. It comes under the heading of an involuntary emotional response.

So the next thing we ought to consider is how emotions come about. Let's therefore take a quick look at this. But here again, let's try to keep our perspective on the other person, because it's their emotions that we want to have an impact on.

* * *

A person's emotions represent *specific ways* in which they are biologically programmed to react to certain objects or situations that can affect them. The affects register as varying degrees of pleasantness or unpleasantness, which they experience as a distinctly felt emotion. In addition to being felt, emotions always have a perceived object: people get angry at, afraid of, or are ingratiated by something, or *someone*.

Of course there are many things that arouse no emotion in a person. So something has to distinguish an "emotional" perception from those which leave them cold. What this something comes down to is whether or not what they perceive is something that can affect them in a particular way. When they're not left cold, it's because they can perceive that the object will be beneficial or harmful, suitable or unsuitable for them. Generally they make these estimates intuitively and instantaneously.[2]

But once the meaning of a situation has registered internally, and the central nervous system comes into play, there is no way for a person to exercise volitional control over the felt reactions that follow. On the basis of these reactions they register themselves as being glad, excited, hurt, angry, or with the same immediacy, even breathlessly enchanted. In short, how they feel about things depends primarily on how these register subjectively.

These reactions occur instantaneously because all human beings are wired in very specific ways. For example, more often than not we don't sit down to eat because we've consciously decided that we need to replenish our nutritional stores. What prompts us to eat is the fact that we are born with nervous systems that make us feel hunger when our blood sugar levels fall below a certain level. The brain circuits which make us feel this way were present at our birth. This is what is meant by a "predisposition."

Now just as forcefully as with hunger, there are a number of other wired-in predispositions which everyone possesses that involve identity needs.

And all of these are triggered the same way, through a person's spontaneous appraisal of the good or bad effects that a given situation can have on their own well being.

This is why no emotion is ever a separate something which is unaccountably added to someone's experience. All emotions, including love, are spontaneous reactions based on how a person is consciously or unconsciously predisposed to interpreting their experience.[3] In other words, a predisposition to respond in set ways is already there within everyone to begin with.

For instance, the incident described in the first chapter regarding what sparked Glenna's romantic interest involved a specific predisposition within her to have her femininity appreciated. This was gratified by the manner in which her companion responded to her well being. And her predisposition to be moved romantically by this existed despite the businesslike agenda of the meeting. Someone does not choose to have a particular feeling. Instead, when a person is confronted by a condition affecting his or her interests the appropriate feeling wells up within them spontaneously, simply because they were already predisposed to having that particular feeling.

This kind of automatic emotional responsiveness, which exists within everyone, is what makes seduction possible. When you want someone to fall into your arms with absolutely no reservations, all it will call for is your addressing certain specific response chords which predispose everyone to react the same way. Speaking rather broadly, the predisposition we're focusing on exists in an unconsummated state among everyone who is not currently in love. This predisposition consists of a hope regarding the status of their identity which is ingrained in them *right now.*

Furthermore, as we saw when we considered how a person in love feels subjectively, this predisposition involves their need to confirm their sense of worth. Yes, a sense of worth is something each and everyone of us can't do without. And you also already know the three specific aspects of identity which produce this incomparable feeling.

Therefore when you become the one who makes someone feel this way, a desire to fall into your arms will "naturally" overwhelm them. And this feeling will grip them regardless of how far they may have gotten in assessing you consciously. This is why whether or not you can win a lover has little if anything to do with your appearance. Rather, it principally depends upon your ability to gratify the particular aspects of identity connected to the other's sense of worth.

This is not to suggest that your observable qualities will have no bearing at all on stimulating love. Clearly, the importance your prospective partner attaches to your qualities will probably be what occupies them at first. As we already mentioned, love arises from two directions; namely, how someone perceives you, as well as how they are affected subjectively.

However, the fact still remains that the other's search for particular qualities is never the only, or even the major thing that will be taking place. Throughout, what they are *mainly* going to register is the affect you have on them subjectively. Over and above the importance of any qualities your new friend may have been looking for, the sway of their subjective reactions is going to be what ultimately tips the scales in love's favor.

* * *

When anyone falls in love, that event is an involuntary emotional response. Whether or not the one who comes to be loved has evoked that response intentionally, or it happens without being planned, the response itself is based on the same predisposition. And this predisposition always comprises the same three identity needs.

This also means that once you have factual advance knowledge of what it is that makes others willing and eager, or ready, vulnerable, or even anxious to fall in love, the thing to do is to direct your efforts along those critical lines. In matters of the heart, this constitutes *the* technique bar none. Rather than acting like the proverbial leaf in the wind, you will be channeling your desire in a way that will lead to success.

Accordingly our technique will be calibrated straight for the other's heart, that is, at the cluster of self-feelings that can leave their heart overflowing with joy, and their mind hoping that you will continue to fill it. So the next thing we have to consider is how to go about getting a line on the aspects of identity which we need to address. This will put us in a position to fashion a tactic which can fully gratify this deeply personal predisposition, and thereby evoke the emotion you want someone to feel for you.

CHAPTER SIX

UNCOVERING SOMEONE'S UNIQUE WORTH

T he major thing required to win another person's love is to subtly compliment those sides of their self-image which we have pinpointed as being responsible for this response. Evoking love hinges on your partner experiencing three positive self-feelings, which puts them in touch with an expanded sense of their personal worth, but one which is completely contingent on you.

Looked at hastily, simply affirming these three aspects of someone's identity may not appear like a sufficient reason to produce love. Since it is not uncommon for people to express the sexual, social, or ideal sides of themselves in a fairly aboveboard manner during their everyday affairs, it may be hard to appreciate how someone's more enraptured states could depend completely on the way these three factors are addressed.

This appearance, though, would be misleading. However regularly these aspects arise during various everyday situations, each of them has an intimate core that carries a special, even secretive significance; more than anything else, they are capable of generating feelings of self-worth. And people don't display their need for this in most everyday situations. For the most part they simply try to protect their ego through a variety of defense mechanisms.

This is why being randomly ingratiating may produce little results. For you to stimulate someone's core self-feelings, that person must actually be expressing intimate aspects of these, allowing your response to be emotionally significant.

So the next thing every seducer needs to recognize about love's ingredients pertains to their almost completely inward character. To confirm another's sense of worth, you must recognize when they are really expressing a specifically personal aspect of themselves. Developing the skill required to reach our goal is mainly a matter of becoming sensitive to the more or less idiosyncratic expression of these three core aspects in a given person.

This kind of sensitivity is important because what is romantically significant about these facets of a person is just what is least obvious, or routinely manifested. While discussing "the need to be loved," Theodor Reik pointed out that there is a secretive tendency surrounding these intimate aspects of identity. He referred to this as "The appearance of self-sufficiency." In Reik's words:

> The need to be loved must be discovered ... because it is often so cleverly disguised and concealed that it has to be found, ... To tell the truth, we are all in a way ashamed to admit that we need to be loved, as if it were a confession of a hidden weakness, or an expression of emotional immaturity.[1]

It's unlikely, then, that your prospective partner will immediately project the core aspects of their identity. Such intimate disclosures usually don't occur until you've already gotten closer. But a seducer can deliberately cultivate this closeness early on by being sensitive to the unwitting ways in which people do often assert these aspects of their identity.

When you begin seeing someone your main focus will naturally be on the general trend of the conversation you're sharing. During the first few encounters potential lovers spend hours talking about their former lives, because this is the best way to show what they are like. The issues raised during a conversation are constantly changing. In adjusting to these fluctuations various aspects of your partner's identity will have greater bearing with respect to different themes. Sometimes one aspect predominates, sometimes another.

But as a rule they will linger on a particular issue long enough where only one aspect of their identity is being asserted. The fact is that everyone gets around to talking about themselves soon enough, not so much in terms of what they think about certain matters, but by unintentionally projecting the kind of person that they consider themselves.

Among healthy adults these projections generally reflect one aspect of their identity at a time. And again, it is not so much the justice or rightness of their conduct that they are concerned with: unconsciously, it is what certain positions they have taken in the past reflect about their value as a person. In those moments the other is being intimate without consciously or deliberately intending to.

So if you respond approvingly when they are projecting these personal facets of their identity, their unconscious reaction will be just as significant as if they were intentionally seeking your approval. In fact, there is an unexpected pleasure derived from this kind of well placed response which greatly speeds up another's willingness to become completely intimate.

* * *

Anyone seriously intending to apply the views contained in this book should realize that just as in using any new technique, becoming competent first requires focusing intently on the basic principles. In this case it's a matter of sensitizing yourself to the three aspects we have identified as producing love. Allow some time to think about each one as a distinct entity, and you will be able to recognize the truly intimate manifestations of these three aspects during normal interactions.

Winning someone's love does not entail doing a great deal, but what is required must be done right. It does not involve indiscriminately fawning over someone's each and every comment. Only when a person is expressing a truly intimate aspect of their identity should you make it a point to be unmistakably affirmative. Such occasions are the axial points in love's biography: it is at these times that your confirmation can have its greatest impact.

Gradually, your repeated affirmations in these three directions will make anyone realize that you appreciate the full value of their unconditional worth. Affirming now one, now another of these three aspects of their identity will clearly convey your recognition of their palpable value as a person. In due course, this will unfalteringly draw out a reaction of love from them.

A strategy of seduction will succeed when, out of your own desires, you make it a point to affirm the unspoken but deepest desire of the other. Seduction proceeds by modifying the insistence of your own need to validate your worth, while expanding your awareness of the other's unmeditated, spontaneous attempts to affirm theirs. Though the immediate results may not in themselves be pronounced, eventually this alone will forge a link that can only be interpreted one way, not in words, but through an irresistible feeling.

It's a little like dancing with someone; while moving together gracefully, you both sense which way the rhythm is going to go. Interpersonal sensitivity resembles that kind of dancing, even when only one of you knows exactly where the interaction is headed. In this kind of dance you will gladly pay attention to the other's expressions of their sense of self, and you should be swept along by these manifestations of how they would like to be known.

CHAPTER SEVEN

MAKING SURE YOUR AFFIRMATIONS COUNT

Even though the kind of affirmation we just discussed is the basic tactic for evoking love, you don't want to go overboard by sticking to that too single mindedly. Sometimes people don't feel passionate about those who gratify their identity needs too readily. In order for passion to develop, it usually takes conditions that would seem to pose a challenge.

Evidently some people don't fully appreciate what they can obtain too easily. Even if it's something important or indispensable, when they get it as a matter of course, they may take it for granted. After an extended study, psychologist Dorothy Tennov noted that most people feel the greatest attraction when they have reason to doubt their partner's interest. She found that passionate love is always accompanied by an undercurrent of uncertainty.[1]

This is generally the case because passionate love entails more than gratitude for having one's needs satisfied. Love is more than a form of appreciation. Yes, the three needs we specified must sense a viable and imminent fulfillment, but passion involves something over and above this.

The additional requirement can be characterized as a desire that has become intense because of the tentativeness someone feels about attaining it. Passion springs from a mental exertion which finally appears on the verge of attaining what is desired. It grows from an anticipation that is nurtured long enough to allow it to reach its maximal intensity.

Love moves us from behind, while also drawing us from ahead. It pushes and pulls us in just the direction we want to go. The push characterizes being moved by a need that already existed within us. In contrast, the pull represents the effect of something increasingly desired just because we are not certain we will get it.

So the basic tactic of providing another person with affirmations of their core identity has to entail more than simply conveying an uninterrupted string of accolades. Since a seducer knows what his or her partner is unconsciously after, the overall objective should be to convince the other that this may eventually be available to them. The mind-set you want to create in the other is a growing anticipation that you will come to appreciate everything that makes them special. But this has to be nurtured in measured paces.

* * *

The classical tactic which produces this kind of hopeful anticipation on another's part is the technique of "blowing hot and cold." This is a matter of alternating your displays of interest so as to draw the other's full attention to the question of your admiration for them. As Ortega y Gasset pointed out, you can always spot a person falling in love by how concentrated their attention is on someone.

This means that you should get your prospective lover to fix their conscious attention almost totally on you. But this exclusive form of attention is not how their mind-set ordinarily operates. Generally a person's mind continuously shifts its focus, so that fixing on anything usually takes effort, or some overriding preoccupation. When things stay the same it has a dulling effect on people's attention. Accordingly, the more ambiguous your expressed admiration gets, the more that will stimulate the other's attention to concentrate exclusively on you.

Ortega describes how people ordinarily come in contact with various members of the opposite sex and their attention shifts indifferently from one to another. Superficial interests, greater proximity, casual affinities, and so on, will fasten a person's attention temporarily on someone. But the degree of this attention will not be markedly greater than what they accord to the rest. One day this equally distributed focus changes. A person's attention seems to stay on one individual in particular, and it becomes difficult for them to stop thinking about this one. Ortega writes:

Initially, falling in love is no more than this: attention irrationally caught up on another person. Should this person know how to take advantage of their privileged position and ingeniously nourishes that attention, the rest follows almost mechanically... Once a woman's attention fastens on a man (or vice versa), it is very easy for him to preoccupy her thoughts completely. All that is needed is a simple game of drawing and slackening, of solicitousness and disdain, of being present and being absent. The pulse of this technique acts like a pneumatic force on a woman's (or a man's) attention and ends by emptying it of all the rest of the world.[2] (my translation)

The growth of your partner's passion will start with their recognition that you can appreciate something of their special value. This raises the possibility that you may come to recognize its full significance. But no single act on your part, no matter how complimentary, is at first enough to eradicate the margin of self-doubt which a romantic context is likely to provoke in your partner.

So if your expressions of esteem only appear sporadically they will have to fix more of their attention on what your subsequent reaction is going to be. This will get to mean more, not because the future ones may be more important, but because their attention along these lines automatically magnifies the importance of your ultimate opinion. In other words, their intervening doubts will deepen their absorption in you — particularly while they're still not certain of just how involved you are.

* * *

Sometimes this can occur without being planned, as when you suddenly get called away and the succession of encounters must be postponed. During the intervals when you are separated by some unavoidable demand, the waiting intensifies whatever longings they had already been forming. By being absent you will inhabit the other's thoughts more insistently than when you were together. When you are not around they recognize that you provide an illusive joy which they don't get anywhere else.

What they will dwell on when your affirmations are not openly expressed or presently available is a form of uncertainty and hope. It is in the intervals between your affirmations that the other's passion increases. When the evidence of your esteem can't be had, the person is left wondering, passing back and forth between doubt and hope, and this is what creates passion. That is why brief separations usually wind up forging deeper emotional links.

But in the final analysis what counts tactically is not the actual cause of uncertainty — just simply its existence. In one case another's passion may be stimulated when they don't receive the amount of admiration they expected after you already showed a strong interest. In yet another it can arise merely from some unavoidable temporary separation.

* * *

Over and above this, there's an even better approach through which you can monopolize the other's attention. The chances of their attention becoming totally wrapped up in you can also be affected by the degree of zest you show toward life in general. If you regularly display a fascination with other pleasures besides your partner, this will indirectly work to intensify their concern with how pleasing they are to you.

By this I mean that when your partner repeatedly finds you absorbed with taking in life's multi-faceted sources of enjoyment, they will tend to view that as a form of competition for your interest in them. When someone can see that there are other sources of pleasure which you enjoy on a par with their company, then their concern about your involvement is apt to get stronger.

Anyone who is about to fall in love with you will be preoccupied intermittently with the question of how attractive and significant they are to you. But the response they want isn't one that grows out of your need for them — it's one that expresses your delight in them. This is why displaying a healthy appetite for life's multifaceted pleasures can also ensure that whatever enjoyment you take in them won't go unvalued.

So you don't necessarily have to intentionally fan someone's doubts to have them fix their attention on you. When it becomes obvious that the scope of your interest is zestfully open to life's other sources of enjoyment, this will produce the same result. Depending on what's more congenial to you — affecting reticence or openly indulging in pleasure — either will result in attracting the other's whole-hearted attention.

* * *

Looked at broadly, the general framework of our strategy must encompass both a giving, and a measured withholding. This can be applied right from the start by allowing someone to realize that you are open to appreciating whatever winsome and winning ways they have about them. Next, you should cultivate a sensitivity to your partner's subjective positive view of themselves, which you then go on to confirm in measured paces.

Seduction, in our terms, is based on fostering another individual's sense of worth. However, instead of being provided unreservedly, as from a therapist to a client, or a parent to a child, a seducer's affirmations should always be contingent on the degree of the other's reciprocity. This means that you should first awaken the full scope of the other's desire to be validated, in order to insure that your affirmations will have a truly seductive impact.

* * *

The next three sections are arranged in an order roughly corresponding with the phases a person must pass through before they fall completely in love. This will give you a general idea of the sequence in which our strategy can be implemented. Also, perhaps at some future time you may wish to refer back to any phase that is then pertinent.

Strong attractions or infatuations can come into being all at once. However, love requires a more involved process to allow all of its compelling power to take effect completely. As this process builds momentum, your partner will experience certain affects that you are going to have on them. Under most circumstances these affects will register without their consciously focusing on them.

But the impressions which you make in their unconscious can profoundly affect the feelings and reactions they will have in their conscious outer life. And it is these subjective reactions which link up to produce the love one person comes to feel for another.

You already know the three particular aspects of personality which play the pivotal role in the unfolding of this process. But because these aspects are not always expressed in the more public side of a person, they tend to lead a largely unconscious existence. Generally, identity needs operate outside of conscious awareness. Accordingly, the following sections will repeatedly focus on the unconscious part of the process, since this is what counts the most.

You will also find that considerable space is devoted to certain pre-requisites regarding love's initiation. This is advisable, considering the momentous impact that a good beginning can have.

PART III

FINDING SOMEONE SPECIAL

He drew a circle that shut me out -
Heretic, rebel, a thing to flout.
But Love and I had the wit to win.
We drew a circle that took him in.

EDWIN MARKHAM,
Outwitted

CHAPTER EIGHT

KNOWING WHAT YOU'RE LOOKING FOR

Before we talk about how to begin a relationship, let's first discuss how strongly motivated you are to seduce another person. The insights you have into the underlying causes of love are the foundation of our strategy. However the form your motivation takes is something that can also profoundly influence how effectively you carry out this strategy.

It's natural to suppose that the strongest spur to wanting another's love is how long we've had to go without having that in our life. This may be true insofar as needing love is concerned. But needing and getting don't always correlate the way we feel they should. In fact, needing often impedes the effectiveness of our attempts to get what we want. The solution to this paradox lies in turning it upside down: instead of seeking what you need most, seek only what you want most. Wanting and needing work differently insofar as getting is concerned: as a rule wanting works better.

With respect to love, being on the better side of this paradox often depends on whether or not you have given some prior thought to "who" you are going to seduce. Having this issue clarified in your own mind *first* will not only eliminate the inefficiency produced by raw need, but it can effect the way you will go about establishing a relationship right from the outset.

* * *

Since at any given time the existing field of eligible singles is actually quite wide, it can make a considerable difference whether you start out with an established idea of your own authentic preferences. Often people don't formulate a distinct picture of the specific type of individual whom they would genuinely prefer to be with. Consequently their romantic involvements sometimes come about simply through chance circumstances which appear to present a handy solution for a very pressing, if altogether natural need.

But just as often, such situations wind up completely disproving the saying that "a bird in hand is worth two in the bush." When real love is what you want to get your hands on, this saying should be reversed. That is, if you single out someone who possesses qualities that are the ones you really want in a partner, there is a direct connection made with your most enticing source of motivation. Someone who is authentically preferred has a powerful affect on the vivacity of your intention to win their love. It's so easy and pleasant to imagine what having this person's affection would be like, that that actually enlivens your determination to have it be so.

The point is that the easiest way to seduce someone is to be moved by them irresistibly. There is a real tug exerted by a person you want badly; your capacity to win them will nearly double because they are so desirable to you. When you are relating to someone who fits your bill, you will get fully in touch with your ability to use your most engaging attributes. Such a person will automatically bring out your most winning ways.

But first you must honestly come to terms with the overblown caricature of attractiveness which you probably pay lip service to with your circle. When you're with a group of friends it's common to take a cue from Madison avenue or Hollywood on who is desirable and who is not. These are supposed to be everybody's official favorites. And yet, though these stereotypes invariably draw our collective accolades, they don't always represent our authentic preferences.

Being honest with yourself in this matter will put you solidly in touch with your own actual intrinsic preference. Then this realistic criterion takes on a deeply personal, powerfully motivating character. By clearly defining your real idiosyncratic tastes, it establishes a criterion that can have full authority over your future involvements. And such an autonomously acknowledged preference will become a powerful incentive that will elicit all of your seductive resources when that can count for much.

* * *

While this may seem perfectly obvious, there is a good reason to dwell on it before setting out on the path we are charting. Sometimes we pursue someone who has not actually struck our deepest chord. There is no eureka, no tug at the heart. A temptation presented to us by an existing opportunity can be hard to ignore. Often enough, there are too few temptations to begin with, so when one crosses our path, indulging it may be hard to resist.

Unfortunately, however, such reactions often prove to be shortsighted. One responds to an opportunity imposed by a particular context rather than to the specific individual who appears to be available. But however tempting such circumstantial opportunities may seem, the only way to fully gain the motivating power that comes from your authentic preferences is by only pursuing those who fall within its parameters. No one has struck this note more forcefully than Soren Kierkegaard in his *Diary of the Seducer*, when he wrote:

> The opportunity falls to one's lot seldom enough, so if it does appear, then it is in truth worth seizing; for the fact is enough to drive one to despair, that it requires no art to seduce a (person), but that one is fortunate to find one worth seducing.[1]

Apparently Kierkegaard was pretty confident about his seductive prowess. In one respect this corresponds with the fact that he was always very discriminating when it came to selecting a prospective partner.

"Attraction" is a force, and the best way to utilize it is by waiting till you are genuinely caught up by it. There is no other way to use this power than by preferring one person to all others at any given time, and being conscious of it. This is why it's so relevant to recognize and work off of the power that attraction can have on oneself. Otherwise you will miss the most potent force there is to seduce a potential lover.

* * *

Once you have realistically defined your authentic preferences, it is also important to acknowledge and accept a universal fact: no one in this world ever has, or ever will be completely perfect. Even the nearest match to your idiosyncratic criteria will inevitably possess certain traits or characteristics that might irritate you. This means that no matter how suited someone may appear, you are still going to have to be adaptable and willing to compromise to make it work and have it last. There is no other way to hold up your end of a mutually rewarding shared existence.

CHAPTER NINE

STARTING OUT WITH THE RIGHT ATTITUDE

T he difference between a person who is calmly looking for a potential lover and someone worried about ever finding one has no relation to the number of desirable people available in the world. That number happens to be the same for both of them. Yet the difference in their attitudes is likely to effect the outcome when either does meet a prospective partner.

Those who are apprehensive about finding a desirable partner are apt to communicate their apprehensions during an initial meeting. Since our frame of mind often influences subsequent possibilities, apprehensiveness can be counterproductive. This doesn't mean that one has to have nerves of steel, or the carefree brashness of a playgirl or playboy. But it can make a difference if you are able to cross the bridge between anxiety and reasonably founded expectations.

* * *

Some reasons to worry about meeting a suitable partner may be legitimate, but it's still possible to see through exaggerated apprehensions and so approach any situation optimistically. The main thing needed is to acknowledge the "no fault" situation which always exists when two people first meet. A seducer should be mentally prepared for certain occurrences which may complicate matters because no one can predict how two strangers will match. Therefore starting a relationship always involves an inescapable element of adventure and indeterminacy.

However, considering the inexhaustible field of potential partners who have exactly the same goal in mind as you do, this is no cause for alarm. For instance, according to recent census figures there are at least fifty million single people between twenty-five and fifty-five years of age in the U.S. today.[1] So if you take the time to think objectively about what's really involved, you are sure to start off on the right foot.

* * *

Finding someone to love and to be loved by unavoidably involves an element of pure chance. When we lose sight of this basic fact we apply flawed reasoning, assuming that our chances of success depend solely on making a good decision regarding who we approach. If things don't work out, we attribute it to bad judgement on our own part.

Let's examine the logic in this by applying it to a different context. Say you are on a television game show and are presented with the opportunity to win a vacation in Tahiti by waging a dollar that you can choose under which of three shells a bean has been placed.

If you gamble but pick the wrong shell, does this mean you made a bad decision? Certainly not! It was luck. Getting back to real life, even when we allow for the difference between losing a buck and being declined by someone we approach, what's implicated in taking a chance doesn't involve your reasoning powers in either case. When you stand to win something seemingly desirable and it won't cost you much, or it won't take too long to find out where the cards fall, there is only one "correct" thing to do, and it doesn't involve how well you can judge what may happen, or going to hide under the sheets.

* * *

Many of us also exaggerate the implications of rejection. Despite love's unpredictability at the beginning, we can be overly prone to assuming personal responsibility for coincidental results. It's harmless if we accept credit when our efforts are successful, but if we take a failed attempt too personally, it can lead us to put ourselves down unnecessarily.

Generally, those vulnerable to this uncritical sense of responsibility start out with a mistaken attitude. Since it is oneself we present in approaching a love prospect, if they don't "score," they attribute it to being undesirable. But such self-indictments represent a grossly narrow view of what's actually involved.

The problem with this overly self-critical view is a failure to appreciate the incomplete basis on which impressions, positive or negative, are made by other people during first encounters. Studies by social psychologists have repeatedly found that most people form first impressions in a precipitous, and far from accurate manner. Actually, "first presumptions" would be a better label for what usually takes place.[2]

Still, despite the absence of sufficient evidence, sometimes people can't resist making snap judgments even though they have hardly any information to go on. Realistically, then, you shouldn't expect well balanced accurate assessments in these situations. Though others often act as if they had a solid basis for their reactions, particularly when their reaction is negative, this is inevitably ungrounded.

Sure, a deliberate overture is a self-revealing act. But if we don't hit it off with a particular person, there is no lasting effect outside that one incident. Making ourselves momentarily vulnerable to someone who will only have a glimpse of us to go on, ultimately has no bearing on our potential future appeal.

We can never know for certain why someone declines an initial overture. Therefore to take someone's lack of interest as a personal rejection is just as irrational as believing that an unavoidable accident is fate's punishment for "being bad." Perhaps that person got up on the wrong side of the bed that day. Or maybe is a "leather freak" looking for a sleazy episode who immediately knows you aren't the type.

Love is a merging which blends two different personalities. Not every combination of personalities lend themselves to such a blending. There has to be an affinity between any two given people. Initial encounters provide the framework to discover each individual's affinity for the other, and when both find this the curtain rises for the next act. So the ideal frame of mind for connecting with someone new should neither exaggerate or underestimate the possibility of finding mutual interest, which is something that cannot be known beforehand.

A genuine meshing of two strangers is always problematical. Nevertheless, invariably *you will* mesh with someone desirable. So the risk you take by your willingness to explore new possibilities is a necessary one. Nothing ventured, nothing gained.

* * *

Beside being aware of the "no fault" reality involved whenever you sling one of Cupid's arrows, it is also well to keep in mind the nature of your target. In this case the bull's eye lies in the other's *readiness* to have love enter their life.

Most people you will encounter who are not currently in love probably wish they were. Though few actually feel desperate about this lack, they know the joy and delight absent from their lives and long to find it. A seducer should never forget that most eligible singles long to be in love.

This readiness is like the electric current in our homes: it is predictably there waiting to be turned on. The more alert you are to this readiness, the more you are apt to hit the mark. So let's take a look at this.

THE NAME OF THE GAME

The main thing that can foster a romantic context already exists within your prospective lover: it is the possibility of their experiencing the personal enhancement that can only come from interacting with a *new, unprejudiced respondent*. Not knowing you (or at least not in this light) provides that person a "blank slate" on which to fashion an enhanced version of themselves.

The overriding condition that sets the stage for a passionate interaction is the *novel context* established when two individuals are first drawn into an encounter. The prospect of evoking another's love begins simply with the context that spontaneously materializes when someone new meets you, or an old friend gets to know you in a new way.

This context is always one in which the other person perceives the existence of a possibility to confirm certain indwelling features of their personal value. What two would-be lovers initially experience is the implicit opportunity for self-enhancement which is presented by the sheer novelty of the situation.

* * *

This is clearly evident in situations where the effect of not having a "blank slate" keeps individuals who might otherwise be attracted — apart. A good example of this is found in studies of mating patterns among Israelis raised on Kibbutz settlements; these studies illustrate what happens when a "blank slate" *is not* available. Researchers were surprised to find that men and woman reared on the same Kibbutz almost never married or had love affairs with each other when they grew up.[3]

But really, this is just what the researchers should have expected. In the Kibbutz settlements children do not live separately with their parents. Instead they are raised in a communal arrangement in which they spend almost all their time with each other. Obviously this creates a great deal of familiarity between them.

As a result, subsequent conditions for the right romantic atmosphere are largely forestalled. The aura of mystery that usually allows strangers to see one another in a light transcending their day to day self-image gets no chance to materialize. Consequently, with no opportunity to view one another in a mutually enhancing way, they rarely marry anyone they were raised with.

But when these young Israelis move to the city — and meet new people — the incidence of romantic attraction is as commonplace as it is anywhere else in the Western world. The presence of new prospective lovers presents each individual with a novel opportunity to be seen at their best. In a sense, this gives them a blank slate which sets the stage for an all consuming interest, that is, for a passionate involvement.

* * *

Once you begin relating to a relative stranger the novel context will bring them a tacit opportunity to integrate a perfected or enhanced definition of themselves. During the first few encounters the possibility of being seen in an entirely new light always makes itself felt. Everyone tends to get animated about the chance to be known differently than they are by their existing acquaintances and friends.

But where is the strategic significance in this? Basically it lies in the attitude you should always adopt toward a new encounter. Quite often we tend to make assumptions based on something we recognize in someone, and act as if it defined what that person is all about. This may prove counterproductive if its carried too far. Not only do people dislike being pigeonholed, but this mars the blank slate you could otherwise be providing them.

The novel context will provide your prospective partner with an opportunity to enhance their self-image. Your appreciation of this allows you to approach them fully alive to this indwelling readiness on their part. After all, as far as your new friend is concerned whatever self-enhancement they may reach for depends on your allowing for it. To begin with you will do well to recognize and make room for this, because it sparks the initial ambiance leading to love.

CHAPTER TEN

LOCATING SOMEONE DESIRABLE

Once you are attuned to the realities associated with finding a viable romantic candidate, you can hasten that event by deliberately increasing your exposure to potential encounters. No one ever found the love of their life while staying home alone night after night.

The day you find someone special, someone who both meets your authentic criteria and also seems genuinely receptive of you, will usually happen by coincidence. But this doesn't mean you should wait passively for that day to come.

To find your future lover, begin by casting as wide a net as you can casually but systematically cover. Most authorities on the singles scene make this recommendation, but omit the "systematic" emphasis. So what they recommend amounts to a spread out, indiscriminate effort. For instance, some even suggest walking to work to increase one's chances, while others list just about every place in the city except basements and rooftops.

Without discounting such suggestions, it seems more judicious to select the kind of locales which are apt to draw people with interests that are congenial to your own. This is what I mean by systematic: rather then being bug-eyed every place you go, select a few specific locales as your prospective arenas. Very soon you will become accustomed to these places, even if only to their general ambiance. Then you can calmly wait for the "coincidence" which may turn into good fortune.

A long-time correspondent of mine showed that she understood this well when she wrote me: "I want to be in a place that makes me feel bright, confident and ready to be sociable. I need to feel relaxed, and I want my partner-to-be to feel comfortable and receptive so he doesn't have to feel like he's on the spot. That's why I note down the places around town where I've felt good, where I've felt the feeling is right. I like to hang out in a place until I fit in there, and revisit it to capitalize on that feeling. When I'm in certain galleries or at the museum in front of my favorite paintings, or out on the lakefront picnicking, I can feel sure about my mood and my moves. There's no question that the sort of person I want to meet is likely to be feeling just as I do in these spots — and that's what's conducive to a successful first meeting and the positive impression I always hope to make."

* * *

Let's be more specific: to be systematic means to use a system, that is, to do things repeatedly in a prescribed way. To widen your access to the field of eligible candidates, so as to choose one that you truly prefer, you have to be present where such people are likely to be. But since you only have a limited time in which to do this, concentrate your time in congenial areas that you have deliberately selected.

Selecting places where you're going to find the kind of person you want to meet should be based on your authentic interests. Any place where the venue can stimulate your participation, even if only as an interested observer, will promote the kind of comfortable rootedness that's likely to help. The point is to make sure you feel at home wherever this locale happens to be.

Some of the more obvious places of this kind might include continuing education classes, workplace cafeterias, political meeting halls, galleries, beaches, single's bars, bookstores, parks, health clubs, libraries, music clubs, and so on. Any place that engages your interests and favors your tastes should be considered.

By consciously choosing certain specific places, your level of expectation is apt to remain positive just by being where you decided to focus your intentions. You will invest those particular places with the promise that any day now, a happy coincidence will happen. Being systematic in this way has a further advantage. When you are comfortable with what's around, with the general flow of occurrences somewhere, this can turn out to be a helpful frame of reference.

The basic difficulty in meeting someone is that the one who makes the first move has to do this with no assurance whether the other is interested in meeting someone. Handling this situation is hard enough, particularly if you are just a casual passerby wherever you happen to be. But when you're comfortably rooted somewhere, it often happens that it is far easier to "test the water." Almost always, there is some information which can be offered regarding the usual activities that go on there, and this can serve as a means to subsequently seeing whether someone is interested in getting better acquainted.

* * *

In all probability by being systematic in this way you will soon be presented with more coincidences than you can handle. But if you've been honest in defining your true preferences, that will keep you from dissipating your most valuable seductive powers. No, it's never a good idea to date more than one person at a time. Once you start seeing someone, you will need all your motivation to foster the kind of momentum that inspires real passion.

INTENTION AND PERSISTENCE

Perhaps looking at this from another perspective will sharpen the point. Having the right attitude toward meeting someone desirable, an attitude that promotes readiness and poise, has two elements. The first is intention, the second persistence.

What I mean by intention is based on what we said about defining your personal tastes. When your intentions are directed at someone who seemingly matches your preexisting preferences, you will feel a justifiable prerogative to approach them. When someone possesses what you prefer, that virtually creates a legitimate reason for you to explore whether ampler affinities exist between the two of you. Under other circumstances this is known as acting with the courage of one's convictions.

When you are moved by an honestly defined intention, you have a legitimate reason to engage someone in exploring this with you. Anytime your goal is to create a loving relationship, you bear a potentially long sought gift for some lucky person's life.

Does this sound presumptuous? After all, not everyone you may offer your attention to is going to be interested. But hold back here. Just what does an initial overture constitute? Is it an assault, or an insult? Obviously it is neither, and anyway people who are already attached and unavailable will probably take your overture as a compliment. Far from seeming like there is anything wrong with you, taking the initiative to introduce yourself shows that you are a realistic, adventuresome person who is used to getting what you're after.

Remember, everyone who currently has a lover was probably rejected by someone before they met their present partner. And what is just as likely, if this partner is a truly suitable match, they too probably turned down an equal or greater number. In any case all that was water under the bridge when they met each other. The point to keep in mind is that those now enjoying the gift of love were not put off till they found this. They persisted in their quest until this persistence proved gloriously and jubilantly worth it.

* * *

This brings us to the second element, which is persistence. What this means is plain enough. You should give more than just cursory attention to finding someone. Selecting specific places that allow you to stick to your best intention is only a beginning.

Only the gods know for sure how many possibly perfect matches have failed to materialize because one of the prospective candidates lacked the persistence to keep looking. I would bet that the number is high. This is why you must persist in your search. There are a theoretically finite number of potentially perfect matches for any given person, so you have to work at it not to miss one of yours.

Again, this persistence must never be allowed to turn into desperation. The whole point of accepting the possibility of mischances, and imbuing specific locations with specific intentions is to cultivate a calm and relaxed attitude. In this way any of us can keep ourselves completely prepared, optimistically awaiting the desired response from a desirable prospect.

Up to now everything we have dealt with applies to seducers of either sex. However, the best way to go about making contact with a prospective lover requires different approaches for men and women. So the following two chapters are addressed to each sex separately.

PART IV

MAKING THE INITIAL CONTACT

Seduction, when cleanly and intelligently practiced, is hardly less than a fine art . . . First, it is the art of *persuasion*. Yet it is more than that . . . It is the art of *attracting*. But it is more even than that. It is the art of *pleasing*, and the art of *satisfying*.

VYVYAN HOWARTH,
*Secret Techniques of
Erotic Delight*

CHAPTER ELEVEN

APPROACHING MEN

Probably by now it has occurred to many single women that the kind of fulfillment we are talking about has gotten increasingly difficult to find amid today's scheme of priorities. Despite an abundance of eligible men, the incidence of real passion appears to have become rarer among certain segments of our population. Though there are more options, and more sensual freedom, yet it's not uncommon to find males whose emotional thermostats are set as if life had imposed an embargo on deeply emotional involvements.

To some degree this is caused by prevailing demographics. Therefore let me point out a basic strategic requirement that is well-nigh indispensable for any woman confronting this dilemma.

* * *

A persisting trend among singles is that a significant number of males have apparently placed the importance of love low on their scale of priorities. Faced with today's economic "realities," they no longer think in idealistic terms about passion. Since our culture attaches an extreme value on upward mobility, we repeatedly hear that passionate love is less important than winning one's way up the socioeconomic ladder. These men claim a need to be "practical" and "rational" about their romantic involvements.

No wonder why, particularly among many professional women, an insidious pessimism is spreading. The prevailing trends that everyone knows and bitches about have infected these women's thought processes and dampened their expectations regarding their own prospects for romantic fulfillment. Everything written about the scarcity of desirable males has served to entrench a pessimistic outlook. Worse yet, this in turn sets up a negative self-fulfilling prophecy.

* * *

Earlier I said that love is not a zero-sum game where one person's gain is another's loss. This is true: real love never is. However if you start getting involved with someone whose priorities make reciprocal passion dubious, real love may not actually be in the cards anyway.

As it is, many women have decided not to get involved with anyone incapable of exclusivity or commitment. But the hard part is knowing just who fits into that category beforehand. This is where the self-fulfilling prophecy can come into play. Those who become *too* preoccupied about keeping a safe distance tend to stay away from more than just passionphobes. Keeping apart leaves *only* a part: you miss as many good opportunities as you do bad ones. By keeping too far apart you can't win the prize.

What's called for, then, is a willingness to distinguish between hopeless candidates and those who may have possibilities waiting to be cultivated. Developing this willingness will put you in touch with a saving patience which might otherwise remain underutilized. Such patience enables you to temporarily suspend the blown-up expectations which otherwise tend to arise automatically in these circumstances. You can wait until there are definite indications whether or not a given individual is at least open to the real thing.

But before this is discernable, the whole thing can be looked at as nothing more than a tentative exploration, one to which you should only attach provisional meaning. This essentially *is* a zero-sum game. But it's one which when need be, every would-be seducer should be willing to play.

As it stands there is only one way to deal with issues that are both indispensable and unpredictable. That is to be both adventuresome, exploratory, persistent, while at the same time remaining tentative with regard to how it may turn out. Should the result not be the one hoped for, you simply chalk it up as merely a transitional privation, and take another turn. That's the nice thing about games: you can play as often as you're willing to, until you find adequate reason to get serious.

To put it bluntly, the kind of realism being advocated throughout this book has two sides. On one hand there is a piercing of love's supposed mysteriousness, while on the other, it requires a saving acceptance of fate's inscrutable hand in serving us the situations we are presented with. Some things can be known beforehand, but others must be patiently scrutinized to see if they are worth our seductive efforts, or not.

One thing that helps to sustain the willingness required in this area is a realistic appreciation of the reasons behind certain males' dispassionate priorities. Because everyone is human, it may be possible for you to look at others' frailties the way you see your own. What I'm getting at is that you can approach certain men with a measure of appreciation of the forces that cloud their deeper aspirations, and keep these from being consciously pursued.

First of all there is a likelihood that many men who have adopted today's casual lifestyle probably didn't do that in a consciously thought out manner. This outlook is generally not espoused as an irrevocable choice. Among most, their dispassionate orientation, even when it congeals into a "style of life," is essentially a superficial expedient. Usually it has been taken up as an unavoidable accommodation to the pressures of their circumstances.

Understandably enough this is not how most single women generally look at such things. Yet what actually confronts anyone who has been dismayed by today's obstacles to true passion is the need to first accept the inevitability of these influences. In terms of your personal interest, here and now, these are not problems that can be legislated out of existence: they are an inevitable by-product of a world-wide economic realignment. Accordingly, the most practical stance you can take is to allow for the social conditions affecting certain people, and focus on their still unconscious need for personal fulfillment.

Furthermore, despite what all the prophets of romantic doom keep telling us, there remains an incontrovertible basis for assuming that most seemingly dispassionate males want to be loved and to love in return. You see, underneath the new attitudes, orientations, and lifestyles, the very forces that promote attenuated involvements also ultimately wind up broadening these same people's need for real love to enter their lives.

By not having really shared their life with anyone, the privation of their need for a sense of belonging eventually becomes unbearable. The kind of superficial strokes that is all a freewheeling lifestyle ever provides inherently gets tiring after a while. This is why most men who have had a taste for casual interactions invariably wind up with a hunger for commitment. Having already experienced the inherent partiality and incompleteness of transient involvements, sooner or later they reach a point where they want the "whole pie."

* * *

If you can grant these things, and feel attracted enough in a given case, the resolvable issue lies in your willingness to go underneath the prevailing mind-set, and awaken the deeper well springs of passion that may be temporarily submerged.

And if it should turn out to be a zero-sum game in a given case, and you can't get beneath the surface, acknowledging what's behind their lifestyle will keep you from blaming yourself for a failure to connect. The fact is that anyone who has adopted an attenuated romantic lifestyle is the one most at risk of being his own biggest victim. What these men seem bent on shying away from is precisely the only thing that might actually bring them true happiness.

However, in these matters the danger of self-blame, or misplaced attribution, is often present. You have to realize that it is not your fault when another person's mind is so absorbed in peripherals that they can't see where their greatest pleasure can be had. So if someone cuts short their involvement, you should assign responsibility to where that really belongs, rather than attributing that to shortcomings in yourself.

But isn't there a contradiction between this kind of objectivity, and the spontaneity which love is supposed to require in order to be intense? There might be, if one has no flexibility. In other words, anyone who has been dismayed by the casual orientation toward love so common in recent years can either continue to expect renewed disappointments, or they can decide to treat casualness as something peripheral that can be changed.

* * *

Having come this far in the argument of this book, you possess a powerful foreknowledge of what really leads to a passionate response. The point I'm trying to make now, before we get to specifics, is that this puts you in a position to handle the added challenge presented by those disposed to hedge on their romantic involvements.

So if you get attracted to someone who seems steeped in "rational" preoccupations, what you can do is give them the benefit of the doubt and engage them along the lines which actually have the most relevance to their deepest fulfillment. Everyone is first and foremost a social being, of a particular gender, with hidden qualities hungering for acknowledgement. What they ultimately want deep within themselves is rooted ineluctably in these three simple factors.

Unless a given man is pathologically dissociated from the core of his own being, a craving for emotional fulfillment will quicken spontaneously when you touch the appropriate response chords. Any man who has not fallen in love, and seems bent on hedging his commitment to love is just as susceptible to having love overtake him as the most naive romantic of previous generations. But they must be seduced.

GETTING THINGS STARTED

You've probably had the experience of being instantly attracted to someone and making eye contact with them, but of doing nothing more than just hoping that something would happen to bring you together. But what usually happens is that the attractive stranger keeps going his way. Afterwards, having conformed to our silent rituals of urbanity, you could kick yourself for not having done something to make contact.

Our expression, "breaking the ice" conveys something of the jarring quality most of us associate with this situation. Everyone gets "butterflies" when an actual possibility presents itself. But at this point your gender may determine some of your options.

Either through cultural stereotypes which are still reflected in current attitudes, or through some wired-in biological programming, nearly all women prefer not to make initial overtures verbally. But this doesn't mean that you can't start the ball rolling if you choose to. As a female you command nonverbal communication better than males, particularly as a prelude to making contact.

Though these options are generally nonverbal, at the same time they can ensure that you get noticed.

Biologists have found that this is a largely female capacity, and have coined the word "Proceptivity" for it. The prefix "pro" comes from Latin and indicates getting in front of an onlooker, in contrast to just being "receptive" without doing anything about it.

Since proceptive female behavior is largely nonverbal its prominence in setting the stage for most initial contacts is not widely acknowledged. However anthropologists who study mating patterns in various societies have repeatedly found that such behavior among females occurs as a matter of course practically everywhere. In fact, and more often than our conventional notions admit, it's actually the woman who usually makes the first move to initiate contact.

That's why when Ford and Beach conducted a world-wide survey of mating patterns, they found that despite nearly all societies having rules of etiquette which deny females the right to make overt advances, ". . . girls and woman do actively seek . . . liaisons with men, even though they may not be supposed to do so" in virtually every society.[1] Evidently, social conventions can never completely bury inclinations that are perfectly natural.

Proceptivity refers to overt behavior. As T. Perper, who has studied the workings of proceptivity in singles bars both in the USA and Canada puts it:

> A woman who is interested in a man but does not express it in her actual behavior is not being proceptive. Instead, she is being passive . . . Only if, for example, the woman tries to catch the man's eye, or goes over to stand next to him, . . . has she behaved proceptively.[2]

Perper defines proceptivity as ". . . a coordinated sequence of signals whose purpose is to awaken the man's interest."[3] For example, the classical proceptive move can be performed primarily with your eyes. Choose a man, then look steadily and searchingly into his eyes for a moment, then drop your gaze. Turn slowly in the opposite direction, then turn back quickly and look into his eyes again the same way for a fraction longer.[4] Then lower your eyes and run your fingers through your hair. This is the closest thing to a real aphrodisiac that most men will ever experience.

* * *

Recently a number of books on "how to pick up men" suggest that you shouldn't hesitate to speak first when the occasion arises. It's true that current social developments favor this more than ever. However among the women I've counselled, I found that those disinclined to make initial overtures verbally, usually wound up faring better than the few who were disposed to speaking up first. Interestingly, once the former became aware of their natural ability to be proceptive, and expanded their repertoire of these behaviors, they seemed to be more successful at getting things off to a good start whenever they chose to.

As you will see following the next chapter, adopting a classically female role at the beginning also has an effect on defining the context. This gives your new friend an immediate chance to experience the kind of "feminine" reciprocation that he will most likely be needing to feel at ease. Not only is proceptive behavior the medium for making contact, but it sets the stage for confirming a very basic aspect of any male's identity.

* * *

To summarize: Despite the widely held view that there's slim pickings for women these days, never forget that while this prognosis was being made, the great majority of women were racking up the highest marriage statistics ever recorded.

And though its true that as a woman you are somewhat hampered by prevailing traditions regarding the expression of assertive behavior, you nevertheless have a real advantage in that very subtle indications of interest on your part will usually prompt an otherwise reticent male to make an overt approach. Any woman can make her presence felt by looking just a bit longer than usual, or by a slight smile, or by preening her hair, or lifting the shoulder of her blouse so that it falls more gracefully, or by walking to within speaking range of an interesting looking male.

Though a few men are thick when it comes to interpreting the subtleties of Proceptivity, the majority quickly get the message even though they are still apt to think that it is up to them to make the first move. If one doesn't respond by making the "first move," he is either married, already in love, or anesthetized, any of which you can well do without.

CHAPTER TWELVE

APPROACHING WOMEN

The changes brought about by the sexual revolution can make it difficult for contemporary males to proceed along well-defined lines. These changes often clash with the masculine stereotypes we inevitably picked up during our socialization. Nevertheless, historically males had always kept most sexual prerogatives for themselves. So according to conventions instituted by our own sex, you're still the one expected to make the first verbal overture. One might say that, by default, you have inherited the responsibility of putting your intentions into words.

Fortunately there's a good chance that the lady who catches your attention has at least brought herself into your proximity deliberately. Still, the most you can expect is just a subtle sign that acknowledges your presence. When such a sign is deliberately extended a woman will be disappointed if you do not respond to her. Most females' preferences lie in the direction of males who accept their established role as the initiator, and act on it with discretion and in good taste.

But what if someone catches your eye who hasn't noticed your presence? It is not advisable to intrude yourself too abruptly. First maneuver yourself within her visual field and allow time to establish eye contact. You can let someone know you've noticed without rudely starring. Glance away when your eyes first meet, but hold them for a second longer the next time and venture a smile that indicates you're pleased before looking away again.

Now even if your interest is well received, chances are you're still not going to get an open invitation to introduce yourself. Quite often a woman who is not at all disinclined to meet you won't show a hint of this, even though she feels flattered by your interest. Whether instilled by nature or nurture, a tinge of passivity comes over most women's behavior the moment they sense the imminence of a masculine approach.

Accordingly, if she did not appraise you first and seemed interested, not only is the first move in your hands but also the second one. Nor does your showing an interest from a respectable distance give her an automatic turn. At this point the grip of passivity is too compelling for her to respond without being verbally invited to do so.

Speaking to an interesting stranger presents a two-fold problem. First, a need to say something engaging enough to warrant a reply. A completely arbitrary comment is likely to seem awkward, particularly to the one making it. Secondly, when you address someone out of the blue no roles yet exist in this situation. So you need to consciously adopt a role that has some relevance to this kind of situation. Let's deal with each of these issues separately, beginning with the question of what to say.

* * *

Talking to an attractive stranger has nothing to do with your ability to speak. You've been doing that well enough for quite a while. Nevertheless most men do find it difficult to start a conversation with an unknown woman. Often this difficulty comes from believing that one must find just the right comment. But by straining to come up with a catchy remark you create a problem for yourself.

Actually the workings of an ad-lib interaction are very simple. We do exactly the same thing that's required here with friends and acquaintances whenever we get together with them. The difference is that we approach a new person with a different frame of mind. The problem is not in our command of easygoing banter or small talk, but in our presumptions about finesse. We think we must say something memorable, but outside of fairy tales hardly anyone ever does.

Frankly it doesn't matter what your first remark is. What counts is the gesture itself. It's the process that's important, or as the old aphorism puts it, "actions speak louder than words." For example, even though our crowded urban centers promote a mood of anonymity, there are a host of things that always warrant a friendly comment or two. This can involve virtually anything that happens to be taking place; a train delay, a long line at the supermarket or the bank, or a book she is reading or looking at in a bookstore.

However, keep in mind that the typical male pick-up line tends to be too directly personal. "Haven't I seen *you* before?" "Gee, that's a lovely broach *you* have." "Can I buy *you* a drink?" The unnecessary weight in all these comments lies in using the word "you."[1] Some women may feel embarrassed in being approached by a stranger. So don't provoke their self-consciousness by asking them anything about themselves right off the bat. There are dozens of other things to say which won't immediately put the spotlight right on her.

Remember, the purpose of your first remark is simply to start a verbal exchange. Once you have accomplished this through some undemanding comment she will find herself engaged in the kind of situation which she is naturally accustomed to dealing with easily. These will be ones that seemingly have to do with something outside herself.

Once you spark a receptive note she may say something noncommittal, which nevertheless signals "I hear you, I'm still listening." But after you've gotten the talking started your next few comments should still lend themselves to responses that are nearly automatic.

For example, if there is no inherent follow up to your first comment, the most mundane question can do just fine immediately after it. But again, instead of becoming personal right away (as in "haven't we met before somewhere?") keep the question impersonal and easygoing so that it provokes no self-consciousness, and so requires no real effort to answer.

Or you might follow up your first comment by venturing an opinion about what happens to be occurring at the time: the service, the wait, the heat, the class, the whatever. Opinions of any kind tend to spark discussion and that's all you really need. Simply expressing an opinion leads from one topic to another in an almost offhand way. Her response will guide you to a topic that will allow both of you to enlarge upon it.

* * *

Even though making the initial connection may not provide you an obvious follow through, this is seldom a problem once you've broken the ice. The fertile tension inherent in spontaneous meetings can move the conversation along automatically. Even a slight halting seldom stops the unfolding of potential affinities. A fledgling connection creates curiosity in both people for further exploration. What is most likely to stimulate this curiosity in her involves the role she probably expects you to play with a compelling stranger who you're genuinely interested in.

FITTING IN WITH A WOMAN'S EXPECTATIONS

The image of romantic love held by most women pictures it as something that begins *inadvertently*. The expression "falling in love" reflects this widespread attitude by equating it to what happens when one falls down accidentally. By picturing the start of romance in this way, most women have a preconceived expectation of how it's going to happen to them. You will see what this involves in the following example.

In a recent nationwide poll conducted by the "Waldenbook's Romance Club," a majority of their female members picked New York's subway system as the most romantic place to meet someone new. The reason so many picked this improbable setting is that people on the subway are doing something other than looking to meet someone: they are on their way somewhere. So if it were to happen that they met a man it would appear to be totally unintentionally. In all likelihood what prompted the women surveyed to pick this unlikely setting was the presumed spontaneity of a meeting under such unplanned circumstances.

What does this say about the role you should adopt upon first meeting someone? Whenever you first meet a woman and she perceives it as having romantic possibilities she will expect to be related to in a way that has a romantic connotation. A woman's preconceived image of how a potential lover would act toward her will depict someone acting out a romantic role.

The widely held belief that love will begin suddenly if she meets the right stranger is associated with stereotypical expectations of how the stranger will act. So women often respond automatically in keeping with the typical script found in most love stories — before they actually know whether they have met the "right stranger." That's why if she perceives that you are relating to her in an implicitly romantic way, she's likely to react as if this is the realization of her expectation.

This doesn't necessarily call for extraordinary conduct on your part. If you do something that can only mean "I like you" during a first meeting, you are acting out a romantic role. It's simply a matter of doing anything that shows you are attracted and interested. When you act as if you've been moved within the first few minutes, this will create the air of a destined encounter.

One woman's description of how her romance began is a good example of this. "I first met Mark in

the university library. Of course we'd both been
there often, and I had even noticed him before, but
he had never spoken to me, and I hadn't done
anything to encourage his interest — I was casually
dating another man at the time. Both Mark and I
liked to browse in the periodicals section, then
begin our studying. We didn't always sit near each
other, and I saw him there a number of times before
I actually noticed that he too was a 'regular.' We
hadn't even really looked at each other, at least not
actively, but I later learned that Mark kept looking
for me, trying to sit near me, and was trying to think
of how to introduce himself for some time.

"Well, a fire drill did it — we had many at the
university, especially in that library — and this one
happened on a particularly cold, rainy evening. I
had nothing but a light jacket with me as we all filed
outside into the courtyard. Mark was right behind
me, and though he didn't speak at first, our eyes met
and he said, 'Lousy out, isn't it?' I couldn't help
shuddering a little as I nodded in agreement. Then
he just took off his raincoat and offered it. I looked
at him, really for the first time, and said, 'thank
you.' Mark draped his raincoat around my shoul-
ders, turned up his collar, and began to talk about —
what else? The weather? How long would the storm,
and this silly drill last? Was I warm enough? All the
usual things one might say, all of them mundane
enough, I suppose — but they started our first
conversation which continued when we went back
into the periodicals section and talked about the
literary magazines we both liked.

"The main thing, though, was Mark's act — it
made me see him as a gentleman from that moment,

and that's what sparked my feelings for him. Maybe some women would have refused the offer of the coat, but I think I responded to the naturally kind way Mark acted in that situation. It would not be far wrong to say that I responded to the old-fashioned chivalry of the moment, and that it was that gesture which opened our romance. It really made the whole night kind of like something that was supposed to happen, a lucky chance that was meant to bring us together."

* * *

Women tend to have strong preconceived expectations of how love will enter their lives. This is why I've stressed the need to be undemanding, and of using objective observations, simple questions, or venturing obvious opinions. Conducting yourself along these easy going lines will allow the ambiance to gel around casual roles which a woman probably associates with a romantic mood. When a meeting is progressing without being forced, or seeming like its been planned, there is an aura that something fated has begun.

The feelings engendered by a first meeting quickly puts the focus on the manliness of the man and the womanliness of the woman. How you respond to this fundamental concern in the other person creates the first definite romantic bridge between two strangers. A somewhat primitive correspondence perhaps, but it's generally how things still work today. So while a seducer is just as apt to get caught up in this kind of gender exchange as automatically as anyone else, you can be just a bit better informed as to what should not go unappreciated at this point.

CHAPTER THIRTEEN

CONFIRMING THE OTHER'S GENDER IDENTITY

hat usually serves to seal a connection during the first meeting involves something both men and women project in these situations, so we will no longer need to make a distinction between male and female approaches.

* * *

Whether or not someone decides to see you again would seem to hinge on a snap judgment. However, before they get to make this decision, something very specific is bound to enter their mind. Almost always, their decision will be based on *how they think you are likely to act toward them in the future.* Now, the only way that your potential new friend can make such an inference rests on how easily they are able to act out certain aspects of their own personality with you. Yes — right then and there — and despite the little they've seen so far.

Though this question probably won't be broached openly, you can count on its crossing their mind. And depending on the way you relate to them, the other may well decide that he or she has a lot to look forward to.

Generally there isn't very much for someone to base this kind of assessment on at first. But since they invariably do anyway, let's take a look at how they go about it.

People are looking for a partner who is on the same emotional and intellectual wavelength which they themselves are on. But on a first meeting they seldom have time to determine this for sure. So they have to make do with the most conspicuous thing there is to go on. The main thing that is available in this connection is often referred to as "sexual chemistry." Taken at face value, such chemistry is attributed to sex appeal, which in turn is ascribed largely to physical appearance.

Fortunately for most of us that happens to be lollipop logic. Yes, it may appear to be the case, but that can really only happen before the actual encounter takes place. You see, once contact has been made, attraction is determined less by what a person sees and more by how they feel. The fact is that "chemistry" is mainly something *felt* rather than something seen.

Now at the outset, the strongest feeling the other person is going to have will be about the kind of impression they think they're making on you. And what has the main bearing on this feeling is their unconscious concern with their own sense of gender identity.

More specifically, since the way your new friend enacts their gender role is the most prominent thing that they can convey at this point, this is going to be their uppermost concern. Accordingly, how you respond to the way they act out their gender is what actually determines how much "chemistry" they will feel toward you.

Let's again address the issue we raised at the beginning of this chapter. As was said, the condition that makes someone want to see you again comes from their seeing *the possibility of acting out certain aspects of their personality with you.* Now we can add that on a first meeting the most telling sign which makes this possibility stand out hinges on whether or not you complement someone's gender identity. Viewed objectively, the overriding stimulus that initially sparks genuine interest comes from someone feeling that the way they've projected their gender identity has produced a favorable impression.

* * *

Normally what impinges on a person's sense of gender transpires outside their focal awareness; but we have to remember that everyone lives in a body. We experience and express ourselves through our bodies. Therefore your presence in another's awareness always conveys an established fact. Your body already carries meaning simply by virtue of being either a male or female body.

Furthermore, your body automatically suggests certain possibilities without the other person consciously reflecting on this. It can cause them to subconsciously interpret the occasion as having romantic implications. For example, often a man's voice will get deeper, while a woman's pitch may rise perceptibly. By itself, this will draw the other to act in line with their own sense of gender.

The difference in how the respective sexes approach each other during an initial encounter reflect what each one considers appropriate to their own sex role. This is why a woman's restraint about getting immediately too familiar may be part of her underlying desire to do just that. In the same way, a man may act gingerly nonchalant precisely because he is very interested.

Again, these are not conscious or deliberate put-ons. Basically they serve to determine whether one is a suitable match-up for the other. Projections of gender are a perfect foil for both eliciting and confirming the latent romantic prospects that exist after just meeting someone. The contrasting polarity which is made palpable by these subtle innuendos serve as a bridge between two otherwise unrelated strangers.

In fact, then, the upshot of engendering romantic interest hinges on your making sure that this intrinsic polarity is experienced. This tends to happen by itself, but it will be reinforced if you make a subtle yet unmistakable reference to the other's gender. By defining something they say or do as being engagingly masculine or feminine, it guarantees that an ambiance resonant with romantic prospects will be ignited.

When the other finds themselves related to in terms of his or her gender, as embodying qualities which make them a distinctive representative of their gender, it will cast you as someone who admires the way they act out this aspect of what and who they are. By displaying that you are charmed by their embodying a characteristic which you consider representative of their sex, you will confirm that this is both distinctive and appreciated in them.

This kind of explicit gender attribution has a distinctly seductive impact during an initial encounter. It produces an ambiance which virtually ensures a future resumption of the contact. It makes people optimistic that if they see you again they are going to re-experience the acceptance they are presently getting.

* * *

One of my former clients (by then well versed in the trenchant significance of gender roles) met her future husband at the pool in their health club. This was a likely place for each of them to begin a relationship; both are avid swimmers who attended the club regularly. Sarah had felt herself attracted to Jake the first time she saw him, but she wanted to make sure that their first contact would last long enough to allow her to either confirm or abandon her first impression.

So Sarah brought an old, slightly defective, diver's watch to the pool and began to try to time her laps with it. This attracted Jake's interest — he had swum competitively, so he knew about the timing of swim meets and lap times. But Sarah was evidently having trouble with the watch; its alarm kept ringing at odd moments. Who would have thought such a thing could happen! Predictably, when Jake saw her fiddling with it, he offered his help. He couldn't get the stop-watch feature of the watch to work either, and so he volunteered to time Sarah's laps using just the regular time functions.

When she was done with her laps, Sarah offered to time Jake's swim, and afterwards they compared "personal bests," stories of swimming events they had attended or participated in. Jake got to show his generous, strong masculinity in a way that wasn't threatening, both with his response to Sarah's old watch, and the way he readily accepted her reciprocal attention as she timed him. Sarah was able to show an endearing weakness which allowed Jake to project and confirm his masculine side, as well as other things she was more concerned about.

Both Jake and Sarah admit that they have a strong preference towards members of the opposite sex who possess the classic "swimmers build." However this alone may not have brought them together without Sarah's implicit confirmation of Jake's sense of gender. In any case, she liked what she found in him, and soon felt that he was someone who could make her feel good about herself. Parenthetically, Sarah has never again had occasion to feign problems with Jake regarding gadgets, or anything else for that matter, and their relationship continues to be a very happy one.

* * *

Let me add a word about identifying the way people project this aspect of their identity. Today gender roles are nowhere as fixed and distinct in our society as had formerly been the case. No doubt this is because most human traits actually correlate more to a person's temperament than with their gender. That is a fact established by several scientific studies.[1] And yet, most people continue to regard the classically defined male/female stereotypes as being appropriate for members of their own sex.

To a greater or lesser extent, most people believe that to be fully mature one has to identify with the sex roles long held to be characteristically masculine or feminine. Embodying these stereotypes is considered necessary for personal adjustment, and so something admirable to possess.

This being the case, it won't be hard for you to tell when this facet of the other's personality is being exhibited. Women have a tendency to act demurely or prim and frilly during an overture, whereas men tend to feign nonchalance, as if they are all powerful. As it still stands, most members of either sex continue to adopt our time worn gender stereotypes as part of their own respective identity.

So since you are no doubt familiar with these stereotypes, when your new friend is exhibiting this make it a point to explicitly allude to this facet of their personality. By responding to this appreciatively you will automatically assume the most appropriate role during a first meeting. This will generate the kind of chemistry which suggests that they and you may easily become more deeply involved. By implicitly confirming this aspect of another's identity you will hold out the promise of *being someone who is going to accept and validate everything else about them.*

MAKING A DATE

Once a distinct sense of this gender polarity has been established, the next step is to express your desire to see them again. But you should first express this desire in a general way before getting down to specifics about a future meeting. In other words, don't suggest a time and place or ask to exchange phone numbers out of nowhere. First make sure that your general interest in getting better acquainted has had time to register. Simply make it clear that you want to see them again because they seem like someone you'd like to get to know better.

The fact of the matter is that for many people your invitation may imply more than getting together on one occasion. For those who look at it like this, it will weigh on their response. So give them a moment to digest the fact of your interest before trying to settle on a specific time and place to meet again.[2]

Lunch dates are particularly good for determining how well the two of you match. Since there probably wasn't time for a long conversation during the first meeting, a casual early afternoon get-together offers the first real opportunity to become better acquainted.[3]

A first date is like an audition, but the part you will read for stars yourself. You can project this best when you're not burdened with the little formalities of an evening rendezvous. With such pressure eliminated, a lunch date can illuminate more of what each of you is really like. When more than a transient affair is the desired agenda, a casual mutual exploration stands the best chance to be memorable.

ENGENDERING FASCINATION AND EXPECTATION

Before we move on to the deeper issues involved in generating passion there is one further strategic point to be made regarding the initiation of a romantic relationship. As a rule, practically everyone has a fairly prefabricated unconscious script of how love should come about, males included. In this script the myth of fateful encounters is followed up by the myth of being swept away — right away. So you should keep the other's interest alive by complying with their established expectation regarding the rapid pace that these developments are "supposed" to take.

Most of the time a relationship must escalate quickly in order for love to materialize. Sometimes a new relationship fails to get off the ground because certain incompatibilities crop up almost immediately. But just as often many people get turned off merely for want of sufficient stimulation. Having begun an interaction they expect a "real" romantic relationship to progress at a rapid pace. Ensuring the right impetus is therefore mainly a matter of not letting the other's interest stagnate once the interaction gets off the ground. Stagnant interactions are like stagnant waters, a breeding place for small but dangerous pests.

* * *

Most professionals who deal with marital relations decry the haste with which many couples get romantically involved. The quickie marriage is notoriously unstable and frequently ends with a need for professional help. Despite this the rule remains that if love is going to occur, it will happen rather quickly.

From a long term perspective the tendency toward quick involvements can seem rash. But from a practical perspective, this is how most passionate relationships will in fact take form, that is, quite suddenly. Speaking tactically therefore, this suggests that a seducer should be geared up for a rapid unfolding of love's developmental sequence.

The fact is that the first date can set the tone for future meetings, so it should be treated accordingly.

Typically the overriding agenda of a first date is finding similarities in anything that can stand as a mutual base. But even at this early stage, underneath the civil interchange, the roots of passion lie waiting to be stirred.

So the very beginning of a relationship is the best time to start acting serious. (Getting serious depends: *cf*. Chap. 11). By "serious" I mean making it unmistakably clear that you enjoy the person you are with greatly. Without seeming to be overeager, a seducer should aim for some romantic sparks right at the beginning.

If this all sounds too precipitous, let me remind you that falling in love usually *is* a precipitous process. Yes, reason and discretion have an indispensable role to play, if it's ultimately going to be worth it. Just the same when love is a viable possibility the sway of unconscious expectation is at its highest pitch right at the beginning. People expect their relationships to start out with fireworks, so do your best not to disappoint them.

* * *

A good way to get in step with love's fast paced momentum is to intentionally assume that your new friend admires you — irrespective of whether they have actually demonstrated that so far. This form of self-suggestion can have two good results. First, by adopting this assumption you create a positive self-fulfilling prophesy. Students of interpersonal relations have repeatedly found that optimistic expectations are the single most influential factor in producing lasting bonds. So always give yourself the benefit of the doubt to begin with.

Next, when you assume that your partner is well disposed to you it encourages you to express a subtly flirtatious attitude that fits in perfectly with dawning romantic episodes. Romantic behavior is an exaggeration of ordinary behavior. People loosen up and act as if they knew each other better than they actually do. So never allow your more placid side to dominate the mood of this first time together.

Though it is possible to develop a warm and affectionate relationship with an individual whose primal romantic expectations have not been met, that would probably not promote the kind of passionate feelings we are aiming for in this book. So while the influence of novelty is still reinforcing the other's growing interest, you want to "build" as much emotional momentum as the budding interaction will bear.

PART V

HOW TO WIN A SPECIFIC INDIVIDUAL'S LOVE

In mutual love, the lovers validate one another's uniqueness and worth. They literally confirm the existence of each other's subjectivity. In love, there is a chance for the lovers to be fully known, accepted without judgment and loved despite all short-comings . . . Love always gives us one more chance.

ETHEL SPECTOR PERSON,
*Dreams of Love and
Fateful Encounters*

CHAPTER FOURTEEN

DEVELOPING EMOTIONAL RAPPORT

U p to this point what we've discussed involves a fairly universal feature of your prospective partner's personality. That was an appropriate starting point because no matter who you set out to seduce, they are going to possess the gender based attribute of identity we just dealt with. However, each person's social and ideal identity has some very distinctive qualities which help make them a unique individual. This means that we now have to concentrate on what is basically different about these more unique features of your particular partner's identity.

When your chosen partner begins to fall in love, he or she is not going to be completely conscious of all the reasons that made this happen. Nevertheless they will have some sense that what you believe *they are like* is at least partly responsible. Each taste of fulfillment they experience will reinforce this realization. They will be led to think, quite correctly, that it is who and what they are like that has stirred your passion. Yes, what they are like.

Let's therefore focus on this, so we can tailor our approach accordingly. In this and the following chapters we're going to look at certain features that

distinguish different people's social and ideal identities in a singular fashion.

NURTURING A ROMANTIC MOOD

Love is an emotional response which gets triggered when a person experiences certain particular
feelings. This means that if you want to evoke
someone's love it will mainly involve your inducing
those specific feelings in them. During an initial
encounter the appropriate feeling to induce largely
involves your partner's sense of their gender identity. Though this usually only occupies a brief
episode, your response to that aspect of their identity will constitute the first major stimulus to their
seeking a greater involvement with you.

But during the first couple of dates you'll be in
close proximity for longer intervals. So a more
subtle feeling needs to be addressed. Probably the
conversation will deal with what you both do for a
living, your overall lifestyles, interests, and current
availability for a personal relationship.

However, on the level where your new friend's
fundamental feelings get formed, he or she will be
getting a sense of how well they can relate to you.
And depending on the way this registers it can
instill a distinct sense of rapport in them. Even
though this rapport mostly registers unconsciously,
its presence or absence is what determines how
drawn they will feel toward you.

Of course there can also be some conscious factors involved in generating this rapport, such as the
intellectual compatibility which may exist between
you, or any affinities in your opinions or values. But

when such issues are in line with your partner's basic expectations, *what creates the warmest emotional feeling they will experience at this time is the underlying affinity they feel in relating to you.* And more importantly, if this feeling is "warm" enough, it will have an unmistakably romantic significance for the other person.

* * *

At first sight it may seem that a truly romantic mood comes mostly from the sexual chemistry generated by a given couple. And yet, when a mood has an authentically amorous ambiance, it is never determined solely by erotic stimulation. An interest that is distinctly amorous has a much broader basis within an individual's personality.

Theodor Reik was the first to identify the unconscious process that underlies the emergence of romantic involvements. He found that just before people get strongly involved, there is one overriding concern operating. At this stage, practically everyone experiences what he called an "unconscious anticipation." In Reik's words, people get wrapped up in "the unconscious anticipation of another person's emotional reaction to (their) behavior. It is, so to speak, an... anticipation, inaccessible to the ego, of the effects produced by (their) own behavior."[1]

Stated tactically, what your new friend is going to be unconsciously concerned about is the impression you will form regarding the way *they relate to you.* But viewed in broader terms, this concern ultimately involves one of the most basic attributes of their social identity. So let's take Reik's insight as a starting point and see how another person's

137

preoccupation with this particular attribute can lead to their becoming more romantically interested in you.

THE PERSONAL BASIS FOR EMOTIONAL RAPPORT

Each individual has a naturally distinctive way of behaving interpersonally. To a large extent this depends on whether their personality is oriented in an introverted or extroverted way. These orientations are as characteristic of a person's behavior as their normal way of walking. We each have a native gait which is noticeably our own. In the same way, we all have an inherent way of relating to others that clearly distinguishes each of us. And when two people begin to define themselves in relation to each other, the way they are naturally disposed to acting in interpersonal contexts automatically begins to manifest itself.

But that's not all; these distinctive ways of relating ultimately have a great deal to do with how much rapport your partner will feel toward you. You see, that person's respective introversion or extroversion doesn't just shape how they relate to you — *it also happens to be what they are going to be unconsciously concerned about at this stage.* Their respective introversion or extroversion inherently defines the distinctive type of behavior that their "unconscious anticipation" is really all about.

Therefore the way their "unconscious anticipation" is going to turn out will be determined by how harmoniously you respond to their particular way of relating. Way before deeper issues have had time to come up, this is how a distinctly amorous motif begins to make its presence unfailingly felt.

Amid the flow of conversation you have with someone, they will form an impression of how their own natural introversion or extroversion affects you. If your response bears favorably upon their concern about their particular way of relating, this concern will melt away and they will start relishing thoughts of just how much more accepting you are going to be. And this will not only promote an unmistakable sense of rapport, it is almost always what determines whether the other person gets really involved.

* * *

Let's look at this from a slightly different angle. Sometimes a man and a woman can find many things in each other that they like, and yet they aren't able to connect on an intimate emotional level. The usual reason for these failures lies in the reluctance people commonly feel about divulging their intimate nature, unless they can just about predict an accepting response. Most of the time people need strong assurances that they will not be ridiculed or belittled, if they are to openly reveal themselves to someone they're just getting to know.

On the other hand, when someone goes home after a date floating on a cloud, it probably started when they began to feel that they'd been understood in a way which transcended the issues expressed outwardly. When this happens it's because beneath the surface of any interpersonal situation, everyone's social self-feelings register the reaction others have to their particular style of relating.

The fact is that the feelings which lie behind budding romantic encounters develop much faster than whatever information is exchanged verbally. So rather than anything said, what winds up being most reassuring to your partner is actually how much rapport they experience. This is a purely feeling-based judgment, made without reflection, like a "hunch" or "presentiment." But it's enough to shape their impression of how accepting and understanding of them you are going to turn out to be. There is a discernable ambiance felt when someone experiences that their particular way of coming across seems to "fit."

* * *

Once the other experiences this kind of rapport, it will have a pronounced effect on their overall perspective. Objective evaluations of your desirability . . . will be put to rest. Rapport produces a mood which eliminates any need for rational scrutiny. Up to then they may have been concerned to discover more about you; but now the rapport they feel convinces them that they know enough. You're someone they can get along well with, and that's what they mostly wanted to know.

And what is more significant, when your partner sees that their way of coming across is well received, they will take that as a blanket acceptance of their social identity. As we saw earlier, this is a very crucial part of any seduction, because the other's social impulse will be seeking a much needed sense of inclusion in this situation.

Now we can also add that the structure and texture of everyone's image of their own social self is based on their inherent way of relating. This facet of a person's self-image is framed around their native introversion or extroversion. That is why your response to this can make them feel a decided sense of belonging which will result in their wanting to be in your company as much as possible.

ADOPTING A TACTICAL STANDPOINT

What I want to suggest now is that once you have a reading on whether your partner is introverted or extroverted, it will be fairly easy to get them to feel a sense of rapport toward you. If you synchronize your response to another person's respective introversion or extroversion, it will instill a sense of rapport in them which is otherwise seldom available to most people.

To a casual observer it appears as if everyone reaches out for personal closeness in just about the same way. Yet if we look closer, both what people are after and how they go about trying to get it follows a pattern determined by their relative introversion or extroversion.

G. Simmel was the first to notice that people approach intimacy with two fundamentally different premises. Intimate relations, Simmel tells us, seem either "to derive from the individual's inclination to consider that which distinguishes (them) from others . . . as the . . . chief matter of (their) existence." On the other hand, Simmel continues, with "many people, the very opposite — that which is typical, which they share with other's — is the essence . . . of their personality."[2]

This difference in what people bring to intimate relations was later attributed by C. G. Jung to the difference between introverted and extroverted personality types.[3] Translated into Jung's categories, those who want what outwardly distinguishes them from others to be recognized are apt to be extroverts, while those preoccupied with subjective sentiments held in common will probably be introverts.

This difference ultimately has far reaching implications. The direction a person leans toward disposes them to desire certain responses from those they reach out for intimately. This means that your partner's innermost idea of what a relationship should be like will be strongly influenced by whether they are primarily introverted or extroverted. So this is what the following two chapters are all about.

But first you need to be able to identify whether your partner is either introverted or extroverted. Identifying another person's intrinsic interpersonal orientation requires some familiarity with the usual attitudes and behaviors that characterize people as being introverts or extroverts. So let's begin by focusing on one of the more easily detectable differences between these two orientations.

INTERPERSONAL TYPES

The easiest way to find out which of these categories your new friend fits into is simply to ask them. Though perhaps not as well known as the signs of the zodiac, this way of characterizing people has been widely popular for some time, and almost everybody has a fairly accurate idea of their own orientation. Because there are no value judgments

or moral implications attached to these character-
izations, people readily acknowledge this aspect of
themselves.

Should this prove impracticable for any reason,
you can generally identify those who are extreme
representatives of their type almost immediately
anyway. You have no doubt met people who instantly display a "taciturn, impenetrable, often shy
nature." These are the classical introverts. In
marked contrast, extroverts have an "open, sociable,
serene maybe, or at least friendly and accessible
character."

Actually, though, the average person is seldom a
"classical" representative of his or her type. If we
were to take a number of individuals, there would be
various grades ranging from extreme introversion
among some to extreme extroversion in others. But
most people would fall in the middle region of the scale.

Fortunately that doesn't complicate things at
all: objective studies of these basic differences have
found that introversion and extroversion are invariably reflected in how a person typically responds to
other people, to their human, social, interpersonal
environment. Regardless of the degree, each type
not only relates in a characteristic way to their
social reality, but they find a way to deal with it that
is in keeping with their own basic orientation. Psychologist Gardner Murphy found that each type of
"individual discovers a means of maintaining a balance between the *self* and *other*."[4]

For extroverts, this balance is maintained largely
through an external frame of reference, that is, in
terms of what those outside himself think or do.
This is what makes extroverts such sociable people.

By the same token, because they relate to many people, that puts a premium on whatever distinguishes them from others. In contrast, introverts maintain their balance largely on the basis of subjective criteria. This is why sentiments that others share with them mean so much. When your sentiments correspond with theirs, it helps them to maintain their balance.

For starters, then, a good indication of someone's type is that extroverts regularly seek to remain in harmony with their peers, whereas introverts seek harmony with sentiments they already hold within themselves. As Harvard psychologist, Henry Murray described this, the extrovert's "taste and sentiments are echoes of authoritative judgments. He chooses what is generally considered good, in contrast to the intr(overt) who accepts only what is good for him."[5] In other words, extroverts are inclined to value conclusions accepted by their peers whereas introverts are more apt to stand by their subjective sentiment on most matters.

Even though this fundamental difference may not always be immediately evident, if you look for it, it will soon become apparent as you get to know a person. For example, it is clearly evident in the way a given person handles problems. An extrovert tends to seek the opinion of others, and is immediately relieved if he or she can accept what they agree on. Consensus with others makes them confident and eager to resume any questionable activity. Under similar circumstances an introvert is more likely to seek a solution alone, withdrawing into themselves to find an answer that is in line with their established sentiments on such matters.

The point is that each type generally shows a consistent style of behaving with others based on how they go about maintaining their balance. This tends to remain constant in a wide variety of situations. So what is needed to make an accurate distinction is simply to separate and focus on what is genuinely spontaneous and natural for a particular person. Just by keeping this distinction in mind, you will soon find several telling occasions in which your partner's underlying tendency stands out in clear, if not bold, relief.

However, how they go about maintaining their balance is far from being the only, or in some cases, the best indication of a person's basic type. Since the next two chapters deal with each type separately, these will further serve to familiarize you with the more telling characteristics of each type. By the time you finish these chapters you'll be able to identify either one with no difficulty.

* * *

Now let's turn to the issue of how one can best approach each type. The perspective we are going to take will be entirely tactical: what we will be looking for is how another person will be most likely to experience rapport, even when he or she is not consciously focusing on this. What we want to put our finger on is *the specific form of relatedness that either type is predisposed to preferring.*

Remember, a person's "unconscious anticipation" of the effect their behavior will have on you is based on either their introverted or extroverted style of relating. So if you make the appropriate allowance for that person's respective orientation, it will prove to be a master-key that can open the deepest cross currents of emotional rapport between you.

Also keep in mind that the object of "customizing" your response in line with the other's social orientation is to convincingly convey your acceptance of their social self-image. Because the social aspect of another's identity is something primal and constantly present, it not only plays a crucial role when you're seducing them, but it has a continuing influence in determining how long their love will endure.

Put succinctly, a person's social-self is what mediates the "comfort zone" which is indispensable for permanence. When love's intensity peaks, it generally settles down on a more mundane plateau. On this level the other's social identity remains the principle source of a feeling that they "belong" with the one they are with. How their social self fares with you is what will ultimately determine whether another person experiences the relationship as being nourishing or draining. So no part of this book will continue to have as much significance once you reach your goal, as the following two chapters.

CHAPTER FIFTEEN

SEDUCING INTROVERTS

T he basic differences which exist between introverts and extroverts have been described by several distinguished psychologists. Among these, Hans Eysenck's book "Dimensions of Personality" has long been considered a classic on this subject. After studying nearly ten thousand individuals, Eysenck summarized his findings regarding introverts as follows:

> According to their own statement their feelings are easily hurt, they are self-conscious, nervous, given to feelings of inferiority, moody, daydream easily, keep in the background on social occasions . . . Their intelligence is comparatively high, their vocabulary excellent and they tend to be persistent . . . generally accurate, but slow . . . they excel at (working with small details) . . . Their level of aspiration is unduly high, but they tend to underrate their own performance. (Overall,) they are rather rigid and show little interpersonal variability . . .[1]

What Eysenck means by the last comment is that when they are becoming acquainted with people, introverts usually have to strain a little. As a consequence, generally they don't make very many new friends. And yet when they do form an attachment it's usually deep and long lasting. This may seem like a paradox, but it's actually a predictable result of the way introvert's inherently relate to their social world. So let's start out by looking into the reason for this fairly typical characteristic. The better we understand this kind of inaccessibility, the easier it will be to get around it.

A SUBJECTIVE LEANING

Jung pointed out that introverts have a strong tendency to focus on their internal feelings. Their outlook is nearly always rooted in their subjective world. Because of this, introverts are very prone to viewing you in similar terms, that is, by making inferences on how you subjectively feel about things. As the former Harvard psychologist, Henry Murray described this:

> In his relations to other people the intro(vert) is inclined to make immediate inferences as to their affections and motivations: he becomes personal and subjective and finds it difficult to co-operate with those whose sympathies he does not share.[2]

The significance that shared sympathies has for these individuals is candidly expressed in the writings of John Cowper Powys. Since Powys happened to be markedly introverted, the following quote can serve to illustrate this facet of an introvert's mindset. As Powys expressed himself:

At the first moment when our temperament encounters another temperament ... the most sensitive antennae and tendrils of our nature ... retract and curl up, drawing inward and curving back like the feelers of sea-anemones ... if this other mind turns out to be akin to our own or possesses something in common with our own, then by slow degrees, these spiritual antennae of our secret being will reappear, and will begin to expand and shimmer in the wave . . . of that other's comprehension.[3]

Looked at objectively, insisting that others have the same sentiments as they do is plainly what causes the paradox we just mentioned. An introvert's deep-seated preoccupation with a stranger's sentiments stands to narrow their chance of getting close with most people. Usually, when people start to get acquainted it's natural to touch on clearly observable, objective facts.

Nevertheless, introverts are so strongly inclined to a subjective perspective, that they are more likely to be on the lookout for any hint of emotional mutuality. By the same token, this also means that if your sentiments do turn out to be close to theirs, they will probably attach great importance to that.

* * *

From a tactical standpoint, the significance they attach to shared sympathies can play a major role in seducing an introvert. In order to provide someone who is focused on this with a response sure to create rapport, you should try to express common emotional sympathies as soon as possible. When you express common emotional sympathies with them, they will take that to be a tacit acceptance of their way of relating. It will have the effect of confirming the acceptability of their social self.

So what you should aim for in your early interactions is not so much for a high valuation in the introvert's eyes, but rather for an unambiguous expression of your own feelings toward practically anything. The sooner you express your sentiments on some of the things you feel strongly about, the easier it will be for anyone who is an introvert to find the kind of emotional mutuality which they have a strong taste for. After all, most people are ultimately more alike than different. So chances are that they will soon come upon a sentiment that is congenial to them.

Naturally the same consideration works the other way around too — even faster. An introvert will begin to feel close to you by showing that you share the same emotional reaction that they are having. Due to the largely inward direction of their attention, few other interpersonal occurrences have as high an impact on their often encapsulated mindset. For example, if they were to express moral indignation on some matter, your expressed agreement would forge a noticeable mutual sentiment.

A good example is a friend who met his wife under circumstances that illustrate this quite well. He had attended a jazz concert at which the sound system was faulty, distorting the music in the part of the jazz club where he and his wife-to-be were separately seated. Giselle was dissatisfied with the concert, and went to the manager to complain. Eddie, too, decided independently to go to the manager and demand some sort of refund.

The manager had been in the process of brushing off Giselle's complaints, but when confronted with two identical claims, he felt obliged to offer both our friends refunds or seats at another concert which he promised would have a better sound system. Our friends both decided to take the free tickets and left the manager's office together.

When they began talking about other concerts, their rights as ticket-holders, the music they loved, it struck Giselle that only she and he had reacted to the poor sound quality; no one else seemed to care. By itself, this led normally introverted Giselle to feel herself strongly drawn to Eddie because he shared the dissatisfaction she was having at the time. Giselle had never been attracted this quickly before, but then, no one had ever identified with her this perfectly. The subsequent concert was their first date, and led to many more.

* * *

Ordinarily people who experience the same reaction to something together tend to feel a degree of closeness, if only momentarily. But experiencing this oneness with another is often an extraordinary occurrence in the introvert's world. They are generally accustomed to being emotional in private. So when you share an identical response with them, they experience a sense of mutuality which is not just unusual, but something of a milestone for them.

Once your interaction involves incidents which include this kind of shared emotional significance, the introvert's need for a sense of belonging will draw them closer to you. When you make it easy for them to taste the gratification of personal interrelatedness, like everyone else, they will want to indulge in more of it.

HOW INTROVERTS HANDLE THEIR INTERPERSONAL TENTATIVENESS

When this kind of correspondence concerning mutual sentiments hasn't occurred, an introvert will still probably continue to pursue the same exact goal, but somewhat indirectly. Yet by being indirect, this can very easily be misunderstood. However, a seducer will be in a position to prevent that.

People who generally maintain few social outlets feel "rusty" when they relate to someone new. The simpler graces of interpersonal congeniality don't come so easily to them. Consequently they often resort to the following device when getting acquainted: they are apt to compensate for their rustiness by trying to exert some kind of control over the interaction.

Keep in mind that this usually only concerns the sensitivity you display toward certain specific matters, and how harmoniously yours mirror their own. It's not at all uncommon for introverts to try to get some control over what they view as being necessary to the emotional harmony of the relationship. Somewhat paradoxically, these often shy and socially withdrawn individuals have an almost compulsive need to influence the sentiments of those they are getting close to when these don't resonate in the same grove as theirs.

Naturally, it may not always be easy to go along with this. Ordinarily such a maneuver could well spark your resistance, since no one appreciates being manipulated. On the other hand, when you realize that their suggestions are merely a manifestation of an introvert's inherent way of maintaining their balance, your willingness to accept it can open the door to an introvert's impassioned reciprocation. Let us therefore explore this tendency more closely so that you can open this door when and if you choose to.

* * *

Introverts and extroverts have opposite ways of viewing the degree of their own influence on events. Each type has a characteristic attitude regarding how they can achieve success in most situations, that is, whether it depends on their own behavior or hinges more on the influence of external forces. As a rule, introverts are strongly disposed to seeing a cause and effect relation between their own behavior and the outcome of the situations they get involved in. By contrast, extroverts lay a greater emphasis on external forces like luck, timing, the influence of other people, and similar uncontrollable happenings.

Now with introverts their outlook doesn't just promote a measure of self-reliance or autonomy; it also inadvertently tends to work its way into their personal relations. In one on one situations introverts are strongly prone to ascribing either the progress or the difficulties in achieving good relations to themselves.

Because they interpret results in terms of their own efforts rather than on the basis of chance events, introverts feel a need to influence events. Yet this makes introverts open up more easily when they feel like they are exercising control. In contrast, extroverts enjoy it better when they feel as if they are being moved irresistibly. The introverts want to feel that they are shaping what is happening, while extroverts want to feel that it is happening to them.

What this means is that during the formative stages of a love relation most manifestations of control on an introvert's part are usually attempts to connect on a deep and meaningful basis. But since they are concerned with subjective sentiments, when a mutually held sentiment is not displayed early on, he or she will do their best to get this response anyway. Though certainly not the smoothest way to go about it, their attempts at manipulation are actually intended as a means of warming up to you.

For this reason the best way around an introvert's typical inaccessibility is to allow yourself to come under the sway of whatever wirepulling they may feel compelled to exercise. A certain degree of deference or compliance on your part, when you're first getting to know them, is usually the best-fitting key to an introvert's heart.

However trifling or briefly, your willingness to let them decide what will probably be some ambiguous emotional issue puts them at ease. If you can accept and go along with that flow, it will soon lead directly to the introvert's more confident and mature interpersonal reaction, which as with most adults, is to share control with their partner.

GETTING THEM TO FANTASIZE ABOUT YOU

Perhaps this recommendation can be made more palatable if we consider what's likely to happen when you follow it up. Another characteristic among those with an internalized perspective is a rich fantasy life. As Eysenck pointed out, introverts tend to "daydream easily."

This is why as soon as a dawning interaction acquires an ambiance of rapport between you and them, it will start most introvert's fantasizing about the greater pleasure that lies ahead. A sense of rapport has the effect of stimulating them to indulge in romantic fantasies.

Why? Because when an introvert still hasn't become thoroughly acquainted, many of their expectations get formed on the basis of feelings they're accustomed to imagining. When one of these individuals is enjoying a sense of rapport with you, it will feel nearly identical to the mood they imagined in the past when they were indulging in romantic fantasies. This happens because both rapport and romantic fantasies produce the same general feeling, so either one tends to directly trigger the other.

Generally it's thought that romantic fantasies only get triggered by purely physical stimulants, like appearance or direct bodily contact. Of course this can happen, but the strongest inducement for an imaginative person to start fantasizing about you actually lies in the kind of mood they experience with you. Experiencing a sense of rapport with you is the most likely thing which will stimulate their romantic fantasies.

Since establishing rapport will lead them to fantasize about you, let's look at another situation that is also sure to make most introverts experience this feeling.

AN AREA OF SPECIAL INTEREST

The most appropriate slant for seducing an introvert is one aimed at their subjective outlook. This outlook makes them feel a distinct affinity toward those who, like themselves, place importance on issues with subjective ramifications. Introverts enjoy playing the same subjective tune together with someone special.

This applies to most things capable of eliciting personal feelings. However there is one area which holds a distinct fascination for introverts. This involves matters commonly associated with an emotional challenge. Though most other people tend to avoid this sometimes vinegary topic, it generally holds a peculiar fascination for introverts.

This is often the case because when a painful situation or difficulty arises, rather than throwing it off as quickly as possible, they usually hold it within themselves and go off to brood over it. And yet this habit gets them used to dealing with situations that other people are more likely to simply sidestep. By not ignoring what is considered unpleasant they learn to deal with, and gradually become adept at handling these matters. This is why they end up with a distinct fascination for issues presenting an emotional challenge.

This is not to suggest that introverts are mainly interested in subjective problems. A fault with any classification of psychological types, including the one we're using here, is that it can pigeonhole people too narrowly. What I'm getting at is that despite their interest in these issues they keep an even keener eye out for anything that can serve to master such challenges. These topics hold a special interest for most introverts because they have gotten accustomed not just to brooding over problems, but to finding workable solutions.

So what's most significant about all this is not the point that in being human you too possess your share of human problems. You don't have to act gloomy in order to establish rapport with an introvert. Rather, what will fascinate them most is how you have overcome any personal difficulties you have put behind you. With an introvert you never have to be skittish about the problems you have experienced in life, but tactically, you should always put the emphasis on how far and in which way you have progressed toward a resolution of such difficulties.

Situations which you have emotionally transcended are what fascinate an introvert the most. Describing how you handled a problem allows them not just to sympathize, but it lets them indulge in one of their favorite activities, which is sharing in the mastery of emotional challenges.

THE LONGING FOR FUSION

As you probably appreciate by this point, a person's inherent social orientation will have a strong bearing on the kind of union they dream of finding. Each type has very specific desires, which when met, move them like nothing else. And yet it's very rare for either of them to tell you exactly what it is that their respective longings make them want from you. So let's wrap up our discussion of introverts by focusing on what people with this orientation generally believe love *should be* based on.

In researching the present topic I conducted what turned out to be a very enlightening experiment. Using several noticeably different definitions of love (taken from the literature of psychology) I asked a number of introverts I've counseled to select the one they felt most reflected their own sentiments. Nine out of fourteen selected the same definition. It was this description written by Abraham Maslow:

> One important aspect of a good love relationship is what may be called need identification, or the pooling of the hierarchies of basic needs in two persons into a single hierarchy. The effect of this is that one person feels another's needs as if they were his own and for that matter also feels his own needs to some extent as if they belonged to the other. An ego now expands to cover two people, and to some extent the two people have become for psychological purposes a single unit, a single person, a single ego.[4]

Since such a large percentage of introverts selected this definition of love, with its strong emphasis on becoming merged with another, this clearly shows us what the most characteristic romantic attitude among these individuals is. In essence, this choice expresses a desire to share their subjective world with someone else. Evidently they have a deep longing to find another person who feels the same way about things which they themselves feel strongly about.

To get a better picture of how this desire might appear attainable to an introvert, let's look at some of the comments my respondents made after they choose Maslow's description of love. Several of them mentioned that this kind of merging is easiest when two people already share mutual interests. They all said that it is best to find someone with similar tastes and cultural preferences. They also said that it is possible for people to change or adopt new interests if this can serve to bring them closer.

But most found it difficult to describe how such a merging of interests could come about, particularly when it doesn't exist beforehand. However, I should emphasize that none of them abandoned the possibility that it could be achieved. As that arch-introvert we quoted earlier, J.C. Powys expressed this:

A lover, (*e.g.*, one who shares Powys orientation) would instinctively dream of some miraculous (meeting of minds) by means of which either your secret illusion would be transformed, or his (or hers) would be transformed. A profound uneasiness would trouble both your impassioned minds until, in the hidden depths of your opposed instincts, some mysterious psychic change *did* occur.[5] (his italics)

Of course most of my respondents expressed a willingness to bring their own interests in line with a partner's. But when describing past incidents where this had actually happened, it usually turned out that it was the partners who had conformed to my respondents' interests. In fact, on my probing, several acknowledged that there had been a need for them to insist in order to achieve the merging they desired.

Bear in mind that their insistence upon shared interests applies exclusively to a lover. As one of my respondents explained, "Between friends differences are taken for granted and make a relationship lively." A friend's basic idiosyncrasies and personal taste are accepted as unalterable. However when it's a question of love, he equated this with a union that "merges two people so completely that they abandon their differences."

* * *

Outwardly this entrenched longing might suggest that they've taken to heart one of our society's prevailing myths about the merging of lovers. However, rather than merely being a naive acceptance along these lines, their desire grows out of the degree to which introverts actually experience another person's needs as if they were virtually their own.

Paradoxical as it may seem, the fact is that introverts are highly other-centered, in contrast to extroverts who tend to be more self-centered. For reasons still not completely understood introverts *empathize* with other people in a spontaneous but distinctly extreme way. Eysenck attributes this "over-socialized" characteristic to the introvert's pronounced ability to inhibit their own impulses.[6]

160

In any case, without deliberately intending to, they often put themselves in your place while taking in what's going on in your life.

When they become close, introverts tend to identify with your need as if its theirs. Presumably this is what makes the prospect of merging with another so appealing to them. Without getting into this "vicarious" tendency deeper than we have to, let's consider the tactical implications it holds for seduction.

* * *

In contrast to extroverts, who just want you to be with them, the introvert wants you to be part of them, incorporated as it were. They get the greatest fulfillment not from passing so many hours of the day or night together, but from having a common identity and living as one. Particularly with respect to the future, they judge every goal as being important or meaningless depending on whether it is shared by both of you.

Many of us might question the reasonableness or even the feasibility of achieving such idealistic hopes. As commonly accepted, even marriage is viewed as a partnership between two essentially independent beings who, at best, work out a compromise between their divergent self-interests.

And yet, while most introverts eventually come to accept this reality, in their search for love there is no room for such compromises. When they are getting romantically aroused they are captivated by a belief that love doesn't have to be like this, that it should be different. In their more impassioned mood *they visualize and long for someone who will fuse with them completely.*

As Maslow described this desire, they want to become "a single unit, a single person, a single ego." Therefore from a tactical standpoint, the clearest sign you can give an introvert that their longing for love will be realized is the appearance that your needs dovetail perfectly with theirs. An introvert's medium of exchange on a personal level is quite inextricably steeped in sentiments which they believe are shared by their partner.

On the most basic level this kind of fusion is experienced when two people appear to want the same thing: fusion expresses itself through a union of wills. So the best way to nurture an introvert's sense of shared identity is by deliberately adopting their point of view with regard to what they apply this desire to, or at least of being willing to share in some part of it with them. Since the fusion sought by an introvert usually involves only those things that excite them the most, once your enthusiasm in part corresponds with theirs you can go about your other enthusiasms without slighting them one bit. In other words, interpersonal fusion does not require becoming someone's clone; what it entails is largely an agreement on priorities, or as Maslow put it, the pooling of needs into a single hierarchy.

Remember, in affairs of the heart no one rates a drop less than what they are willing to share with you. At the same time, this willingness on your part is the main thing needed for you to sweep anyone who is an introvert away.

* * *

As we said at the outset, anyone seeking love will be looking for someone who responds to them in a certain way. Now, with the foregoing insights at your disposal, you should have a general picture of what an introvert will be looking for in this regard.

In large part this will require that you harmoniously resonate many of your partner's subjective sentiments. In turn this kind of resonance will gradually build a broad enough spectrum of shared personal sentiments, one which can serve to define both of you as having a mutually held identity. This, as we just saw, will provide most introverts with the only sense of belonging that they dream and hope for, and so can really thrive on.

Frankly this may require a distinct effort on your part, particularly if you happen to be extroverted. As we will see in a moment, this kind of subjective resonance does not come automatically to those who are more strongly focused on what's going on outside themselves.

So you would be called upon to make a deliberate determination to give your partner the kind of personal resonance which he or she is predisposed to desiring. And yet, considering the rewards which can be expected from a successful seduction, this could make a commitment along these lines worth whatever effort it might entail.

CHAPTER SIXTEEN

SEDUCING EXTROVERTS

T he extent to which extroverts use the external field as a source of reference for their behavior is the most distinguishing feature of their mind-set. They are acutely conscious of the activities going on outside themselves, and so are mainly interested and responsive to these. Most of the time extroverts will respond to a situation directly; they tend to handle its details somewhat extemporaneously, rather than relying on preexisting sentiments about how things should be.

This is why, in contrast to the importance which introverts place on emotional fusion, most extroverts would probably look at that goal as being way too ephemeral. Rather than weaving their dreams of love out of internally fixed sentiments, extroverts weave their romantic hopes largely around outwardly perceived events. Especially during the early stages of a relationship, you are apt to find an extrovert avidly pursuing the wide array of stimulation that life has to offer.

So with an extrovert, concerning yourself with the issue of shared subjective impressions is not the way to go. Instead a seducer has to address the implications surrounding the palpable stimulation and excitement of overt events. That is the hallmark of an extrovert's interest. In place of an "inner sanctum," they will want to embrace the pleasures that can be derived from life's overt stimulation.

Their absorption with the external field disposes extroverts to seek a steady flow of changing experiences to keep things interesting. Typically they are very open to change, excitement, and fresh stimulation. In addition to this, most extroverts also tend to be impulsive, or at least quite ready to respond to unknown conditions with enthusiasm. As Jung summarized this, "Whatever is unknown appears alluring."

This strong penchant for getting immersed in all sorts of activities often finds them having to improvise new and untried courses of action quite hastily, particularly when it's an unfamiliar pursuit. However, right along with this impulsiveness they are also highly sensitive to slight slips, inaccuracies, or any kind of strained effort, especially in public.

RAPPORT AND AFFECTABILITY

Here, in this "impulsive" characteristic, we find our first tactical opening for seducing an extrovert. The reason for this is that people who are even slightly impulsive generally possess a high level of affectability. By "affectability" I mean the degree to which a person is directly influenced by the immediate affects they are experiencing at any given moment. (We could also refer to this quality as "impressionableness," since it is perhaps more familiar; however "affectability" lays a greater stress on being affected emotionally and this is what we're concerned with).

Naturally, everyone reacts to whatever is taking place. But there is a noticeable difference in the immediate impact this has upon extroverts as compared to introverts. As William McDougall first pointed out, extroverts are more liable ". . . to be checked and diverted from their course of action, and to be prevented from returning to any similar line of action, by the pain of difficulty and thwarting encountered; and to be more strongly sustained in their striving, and stimulated to further and renewed efforts along similar lines, by the pleasure that comes with progress and success."[1]

In keeping with this quality, when an extrovert gets into a novel situation he or she is very likely to rely on feedback from those around them. They need repeated signs of how well they are handling things. This is what makes an extrovert's strong affectability the royal road to providing them a response which is perfectly tailored to evoke rapport.

In a stronger than average way, an extrovert's sense of well-being depends on how well their performance "comes off" in their audience's estimation. As Jung observed, extroverts consider the main reason for their well-being as something contingent on the reactions of those in their immediate environment. So while their attention will be absorbed in the activity taking place, their greatest enjoyment comes not so much from their accomplishments but from being seen by another as performing in an effective manner.

That is why an extrovert's "affectability" is nearly always available as an access to generating emotional rapport with them. Such opportunities are quite common because in keeping with their impulsive nature they quite frequently get involved in activities where they can use direct encouragement. In a sense, they are more or less accustomed to being out on a limb. So when you take into account this proclivity for doing things extemporaneously, and add that they are highly affected by the thwarting or support they encounter, it's obvious that endorsing their efforts will be more than mildly welcomed.

THE CONFIRMATORY SHADOW

Some readers may find this recommendation a bit trite. I could not argue with that. However despite its less than sophisticated overtones, this line of approach remains the most perfectly suited to ingratiate anyone with an extroverted mind-set. Perhaps the appropriateness of this approach will stand out more clearly if we look at how the famous British author, H. G. Wells (a self-described extrovert) revealed his sentiments on this issue.

In the previous chapter John Cowper Powys' writings on love served to illustrate two characteristic biases of his introvertedness. In the same way, Wells affords us an incomparably candid look at the workings of an extrovert's psyche. Here are his words on what love meant to him and by extension, to those who share his orientation:

Jung calls the figure we make of ourselves in our imaginations for the purpose of behavior, the Persona (*e.g.* what we are referring to as the social-self) . . . this Persona is never sure of itself and always hungry for confirmation of its cherished insecure self-respect. ... (a) Lover is the Persona-Shadow; the shadow that makes the Persona seem solid and real ... Essentially it is confirmatory. We are all seeking that confirmatory shadow. *The essential craving is not for completion but endorsement.* One of the great functions of a lover is to tell us we are "all right" to keep us feeling we are "all right," ... The executives of big businesses find it necessary to sustain their will through many of their operations by keeping about them a number of subordinates, cooing approval, their 'Yes-men.' These hold the principal to his determined course. Well, this Lover-Shadow of mine so earnestly sought and so indispensable to mental contentment, is for all practical purposes nothing more than the Yes-Man or Yes-Woman of the Persona ... I don't think the human being is built, (*e.g.*, those who share Wells' outgoing nature) I don't think the Persona is so constructed, as to carry on without a Yes-Man or Yes-men ...[2] (my italics)

* * *

Looked at objectively, what Wells' self-revealing words serve to illustrate is how sensitive extroverts are with respect to their role as protagonists in ongoing situations. Repeatedly they become immersed in what is taking place, so they want to play an active and effective role. But because they derive their sense of well being from the reflected appraisals gained in social interaction, extroverts routinely carry their self-esteem on their sleeve, as it were.

Therefore their major preoccupation involves a constant exposure to the possibility of negative reflections on their overt actions. Given, then, that much of an extrovert's activities are strongly influenced by his or her need for social approval, and that they easily get caught up in what is taking place around them, they can be profoundly moved by any sort of encouragement or praise. The effect of encouraging their performance, or the merit of their having undertaken something, enhances their feelings in a singular fashion.

Such encouragement comes through best when you recognize and comment on the effort, interest, or the concern they put into a venture, rather than waiting to judge its final outcome. For example, if they meet with some mishap we would not say "You still haven't gotten it right," but rather, "You improved your performance since the last time." Encouragement requires that we view the other as an effective protagonist instead of holding them up to rigid standards. It relates to current initiatives and prospects, rather than alluding to ultimate goals: it focuses on means, not ends. By encouraging someone you provide feedback which validates the value of the effort they have actually ventured.

Seducing an extrovert is in large part a matter of making yourself a constant source of positive feedback, or as Wells put it, a confirmatory shadow. Rapport can be easily established simply by providing the encouragement which allows them to persevere in their extemporaneous endeavors. Since their self-feelings are tied directly to a radar-like process focused to bounce off other people, even the slightest encouragement helps them deal with the external field with ease and assurance. This is why

169

no other gambit, no matter how sophisticated, has a greater bearing on an extrovert's rapport with you.

TOGETHER BUT DISTINCT

A person's extroversion not only determines how much they depend on feed-back from you, it also shapes the nature of the attachment or union they want to establish. When two people interact in a personal context the emergence of rapport impels them to want to be together on a continuing basis. As this desire takes hold, both introverts and extroverts will seek to establish some form of union with you. Now the main thing to remember is that each individual's style of relating is matched by a corresponding attitude as to what such a union should entail.

As we noted earlier, introverts view a union in terms of merging identities and becoming a kind of single unit with another. This vision of union puts a premium on sameness, particularly with regard to emotions, aesthetic attitudes and overall sentiments. We could call this a desire for a union that resonates with similarities.

By contrast, an extrovert will place little stock in the existence of similarities. For the most part the sort of union sought by an extrovert is one in which they and you are, and stay different. Such unions are no less binding or close but the connection consists of the complementary links between two separate and distinct individuals.

But don't misunderstand; this doesn't mean that extroverts only want to form close bonds with those who are completely opposite to themselves. The point is that regardless of how similar or dissimilar you may be, an extrovert will envision a relationship mainly in terms of a *complementary union.*

You can get an idea of how extroverts conceive this kind of union from the experiment I mentioned earlier. When I asked extroverts to choose the description of love they considered most appealing, a significant majority chose the following metaphorical phrases written by Kahlil Gibran:

> Love possesses not nor would it be possessed
> . . . Let there be spaces in your togetherness
> . . . let the winds of the heavens dance between
> you . . . Fill each others cup but do not drink
> from one cup . . . Even as the strings of a lute
> are alone though they quiver with the same
> music . . .[3]

In selecting Gibran's description, my respondents expressed a clear reluctance to relinquish their independence and individuality. This suggests that regardless of how many interests they may share with you, extroverts will probably want to keep some aspects of their life separate.

On further questioning several of these respondents described close relationships as consisting of two people reflecting each other's strengths and complementing one another's interests. Usually this works out in real life as two people supplementing each other's weak points. For example, with a partner who is at risk of turning into a hermit, an extrovert will probably save them from that fate. Or perhaps an extrovert needing to shore up their independent judgement will find a handy model to imitate, if they are with an introvert.

This form of togetherness can be likened to the relationship between members of a team where each performs a distinct function but all have a complementary purpose. This is apparently as much oneness as extroverts feel is possible. So from a tactical perspective, keep in mind that it is probably as much as they will desire. In a word, extroverts are not disposed to giving up their separate identity, so suggesting this is not recommended.

DISTINCT BUT TOGETHER

Despite this consideration let's not forget that extroverts possess a strongly sociable nature. Even with their inclination to uphold their distinct identity they remain at one and the same time the most gregarious people. Perhaps the significance they attach to togetherness can be illustrated by quoting H. G. Wells again.

In this particular instance Wells' attempt to grapple with the question of love is contained in a thinly-veiled intellectual autobiography titled, *The Anatomy of Frustration*. This accounts for his awkward attempt to attribute his ideas to a fictional "he" in the following passages.

The gist of it all is that he felt lonely and did not like to feel lonely; it lowered his efficiency. And he realized that this ache of *loneliness* which colored so many of his mental states and accounted for much of his practical ineffectiveness was not peculiar to himself, that to have these moods is the common lot of actively intelligent people in the world today

. . . What is it that is sought to assuage this loneliness? . . . The ordinary way of putting it is that we want to love and be loved . . . the active modern type of mind demands and *needs response* (from others) . . . it cannot carry on life effectively without response . . . Love is a giving and a taking, and from both aspects it breaks down the *isolation* of the self . . .[4] (my italics)

As we might have expected, those with the most sociable personalities see loneliness as something unbearable. Consequently they look for a lover to be a shadow that can blot out loneliness. But keep in mind that despite needing continuous "response," this concern will be balanced by the extrovert's desire to maintain their separate identity. So while they will want to be with you as much as possible, as Gibran wrote, you should allow for spaces in your togetherness.

WHY EXTROVERTS MANIFEST THIS PARADOX

Considering that extroverts are basically outgoing and sociable their disinclination to merge totally with a lover may seem contradictory. After all an extrovert's gregariousness is perhaps their most distinguishing characteristic. To understand why these opposed tendencies often co-exist in the same person we have to look at the issue of personal individuality, and the significance it can take on as something to contend with.

In a society such as ours, where individuality is ranked as a holy grail and everyone prides themselves on how self-sufficient and individualistic they are, it's not uncommon for extroverts to become overly preoccupied with living up to these expectations. Because they are strongly influenced by the tenor of the times, extroverts tend to become highly sensitive about their own sense of separate identity. Consequently once they've formed a set boundary of their distinct identity, preserving this becomes a psychological priority.

But this is not the easiest thing for someone with an externalized frame of reference to accomplish. Although individuality is largely defined by behavior, extroverts also rely on the feedback which they get from their partner to define their distinct identity. Therefore the partner has to remain a separate entity in order to serve this function.

When you're using the other's response as the medium for defining your own individuality, you can't merge with them completely and still use them to delineate your individual identity. They have to remain separate in order for you to have a relevant boundary to define yourself from. This accounts for the paradox that though highly dependent on social response, an extrovert feels obliged to attenuate the nature of his or her merging with others, including a lover.

I have emphasized this point because it presents one of the most common obstacles to enduring relationships between introverts and extroverts. Too often the passion sparked by two oppositely oriented individuals leads each to seek a consummation solely in line with their own vision of perfect harmony.

Almost automatically, all of us tend to believe that another's psychology is the same as our own.

Ultimately, it actually is. As H. S. Sullivan correctly insisted, we are all more alike than otherwise. Yet concerning the architecture of our romantic unions, which we all long for with equal fervor, the blueprints held by introverts and extroverts are so divergently stenciled in each one's respective psyche that these differences warrant both our respective understanding as well as our mutual respect. The fact, as I already mentioned, is that if one is seeking the ultimate reward of permanence it requires a conscientious, seductive decision to allow for those longings which differ structurally from one's own.

FINDING UNIQUENESS

In addition to the bearing it has on the kind of relationship extroverts are most comfortable with, the importance they attach to keeping a separate identity carries with it a major tactical opening. The key to romance with an extrovert rests on the way he or she hopes you will see them. With rare exceptions, this centers around the quality of uniqueness. In the same compelling way that sharing in an introvert's identity seals their love, an extrovert's passion spins off of your appreciation of those things which make them unique. So let's take a good look at this.

* * *

Not long ago being an average person was nothing to be ashamed of. The more people thought they had in common, the easier they found it to live among one another. But after three decades of "hip," "I," "me" and "number one" head trips, all that has changed. Today being labelled "average" would make most of us feel like second class citizens.

Unfortunately this abhorrence of being considered average weighs more heavily on those who are already preoccupied about their individuality. In fact it generally leads them to put a high premium on being considered unique.

However in our day this is no easy matter. Modern societies assign most individual's roles that are held by other people too. Then modern industry manufactures symbols of distinctiveness such as Gucci purses a thousand at a time. Or a young person wanting to be "different" goes to the neighborhood hairstylist for the latest cut and finds a line of others with the same intention stretching halfway down the street.

In these and innumerable other ways, everyday emblems of uniqueness are getting harder to find. No one bears a greater burden in our increasingly homogenized culture than those who rely on visible proofs of uniqueness to confirm their individuality. Though you don't have to be extroverted to get caught up in the quest for uniqueness, more often than not it does work out that way.

Relatively speaking it's easier for introverts to maintain a sense of separate individuality without relying on outside cues. Given their habitual internalized perspective introverts are constantly in touch with their own needs, feelings, and attitudes toward themselves. In this way they automatically maintain a sense of separate identity as distinct from others. By contrast, a person with an active, outgoing mind has to rely on outside cues to substantiate their singular distinctiveness.

Therefore, the thing to remember is that since extroverts are more tuned into outside feedback to maintain their sense of individuality anyway, this places you in a very seductive position. Again, this provides you with a key which can fit an extrovert's heart quite perfectly. The way they will most vividly register that they appeal to you involves how much you appear to be taken by their uniqueness.

Any aspect of an extrovert's personal make-up which lends itself to being "singled out" as uncommon can serve this purpose. Since they are strongly affected by outside frames of reference, a remark like, "I've never seen it done that way — that's pretty unusual," will show that you are impressed by the palpability of their distinctiveness. When your response to an extrovert serves to differentiate her or him as a unique individual, the rapport they will feel for you is going to be poignant.

But don't extroverts get this all the time from their wide circle of friends? No, not as a rule. True, most friends are a good source of personal validation; but the equality that usually prevails among a group of friends makes it difficult for them to satisfy their craving for uniqueness in those situations. Accordingly, the possibility of becoming the most important person in your life is particularly irresistible for extroverts. Despite having many friends, an extrovert will seldom hesitate when love appears on the horizon.

At some point, then, to draw out an extrovert's full passion you should not only let them know you appreciate their uniqueness, but you should make them feel that they are irreplaceable. At the right time you can insist that you have a specific need which *they alone* will be able to fulfill.

The following story is a good illustration of the impact that feeling irreplaceable can have on an extrovert. Robin, a twenty-nine year old former client of mine had been dating a very outgoing man who worked as a physical fitness consultant. After seeing him steadily for three months it became evident that they were very suited for each other. One weekend Arnold stayed over at his brother's apartment, baby-sitting his two nieces. Robin spent that weekend helping Arnie and it served to cinch her opinion of him. Arnie had a way with the two young girls that was at once protective and giving. Robin saw that he was someone she could build her future with.

But when she started giving him clear cues that they should think seriously about marriage, he suddenly began pulling back with vague allusion to how good things were the way they were. Though he never actually acted like he'd lost interest, something was plainly making him back off. Finally confronted with Robin's justifiable puzzlement, he told her the real reason. It seems Arnold was tentative about making a commitment because he had been left holding the bag in his last two relationships.

Since Robin felt that they had enough going well between them that was worth keeping, she decided to deal with Arnie's difficulty by addressing it constructively. From work she and I had completed a year earlier, Robin knew that the solution to this type of quagmire (both in oneself and in dealing with others) often lies in providing a ready made remedy which washes out the problem, rather than confronting it frontally with potentially divisive debates. Besides, she knew that Arnie's extroversion made him very uncomfortable when focusing on subjective matters.

Arnold's inability to fully commit was the results of what he was conditioned to expect, namely renewed disappointment. So all he needed was a high powered dose of something else — for something good to materialize — to wash out his wounded expectancy. The strategy Robin used to put Arnie's reservations to rest is as thoughtfully seductive as it is simple.

She had been a yo-yo dieter in the past, something she had to prove to Arnie with an old photograph. So when she sought his help to take off a few pounds she'd ostensibly put on, he gladly showed her an aerobic regimen that he guaranteed would permanently solve the problem. Robin thanked Arnie, but said it wouldn't work because she'd never been able to keep up exercise for more than a few days. Arnie promised that if she followed his instructions that wouldn't happen this time. Somewhat reluctantly, she agreed to try.

A week later, as miraculously as it had appeared, the weight disappeared. Then each subsequent time they were together Robin's enthusiasm over Arnie's expertise never failed to stress how indispensable his continued guidance was for her. Gradually, (she was in no hurry) imperceptibly, (she never mentioned marriage again) her repeated affirmation of his irreplaceable place in her life removed the vestige of his old wound. And any remaining reservations were thoroughly washed out when he placed the ring on her finger and they both said "I do."

An extrovert, perhaps just a tinge more than others, will want to feel that he or she has an irreplaceable priority in your life. Because everyone interprets another's attentions as something inspired by their particular qualities, conferring this priority on them will substantiate the distinctiveness of an extrovert's uniqueness more than anything.

* * *

Another slant that works to affirm an extrovert's uniqueness is to identify the personal significance which they themselves attach to what they tell you. You have to grasp the subjective meaning of what they say, the personal meaning that whatever they are discussing *has for them.* Usually people implicitly express how they feel about the events they are describing. But generally we pay more attention to the events described than to the meaning the other attaches to them. This is natural because a conversation is normally kept flowing by reference to concrete details.

Still, if you "listen" for it, you will easily catch the personal meaning behind what the other tells you. Then you can express your understanding and acceptance of how they feel about whatever it is. Sometimes all this takes is saying, "I can see why you feel that way." The tactical implication here with respect to extroverts is that by acknowledging and echoing the personal significance behind what they are expressing, you will also differentiate that person's individuality vis-a-vis the situation they are referring to.

Nothing is more individual than how someone feels about what they elect to tell you. So when they express their particular slant on some situation or event, this personal meaning is also delimiting their separate individuality. Therefore by acknowledging the appropriateness of his or her slant on something, you will indirectly substantiate the distinctiveness of their personality.

Of course this often happens on its own between those getting close. Perhaps this is why extroverts are generally the easiest people to get along with. In all likelihood such will be the case so long as you remember three things: first, endorse their enactments through positive feedback. Next, stick to alliances and not mergers. And finally, let them know that they are not only a one and only, but could easily be your one and only.

* * *

There is an old Spanish proverb which says, "Faces we see, hearts we know not." While this rings well, it's really no more than a handy cop-out. People are not so inscrutable, or all that complex. They just want to attain their own personal version of contentment; but what always lies in their heart is a specific definition of how to get this.

After reflecting on the observations in this and the preceding chapter, you should now have a basic picture of the kind of definition held by either an introvert or an extrovert. So long as you remember that your prospective lover will have a distinctive orientation along the lines we have discussed, you will be in a position to customize your approach in a way that quickly leads from rapport to passion.

However, to secure a truly impassioned response, one further aspect of your future lover's identity requires special consideration. The final phase your future lover must pass through before they surrender completely to love's binding destiny will have one central theme: this involves how many of their superior qualities you will come to see, enjoy, and acknowledge.

Before that person sets you up as the center piece of their existence you have to discover some of their finer attributes. You must show that you are moved because you admire and value these virtues of theirs. And you must appear to be distinctly aware of their inordinate value.

CHAPTER SEVENTEEN

ON THE BRINK OF LOVE

O nce you've aroused someone erotically by confirming their sexual identity, and gotten them to feel that they belong with you because you've made it easy for them to relate to you naturally, only one other move is required. What you need to do to guarantee the full emotional reaction we are aiming for involves your partner's self-ideal.

But this is usually something hidden inside a person. Yes hidden: people don't like to talk about things that can come off as being self-glorifying. Accordingly, they seldom wear their ideal self-image on their sleeve. This is generally kept under tight wraps.

And yet the fact remains that anyone falling in love will be drawn on by the vaguely sensed promise of an impending consummation. Even when love hasn't been avowed yet, your partner will be kept on the romantic quest hoping that everything they are, including what they are capable of being, will be recognized and admired by you. Once your partner thinks that they may be about to fall in love, he or she is going to be gripped by a desire to validate the ideal facet of their identity.

Though this validation won't be sought openly, it's likely to be what dominates their longings at this point. How can we be sure? Because the highest and most problematical aspect of a person's identity almost always comes to the fore during the episodes which take place just before they fall in love. Anyone who is close to achieving what is optimal in life feels compelled to bring forward what is optimal in themselves; only by having their best confirmed will they be sure that they deserve to achieve so much.

* * *

But since these deeply intimate hopes are usually held down by a certain reticence, its very likely that this desire will be obliged to work itself out inconspicuously. More specifically, they are apt to seek a validation of their self-ideal through a somewhat roundabout process.

This means that you can expect that when your partner reaches this point they will probably undergo a crisis centered around your appreciation of what is best in them. A person on the brink of love needs to be seen in ways that acknowledge them as being a cut above the average, and hence worthy of being loved. Again, it's not likely for them to seek this out directly. Ordinarily a person on the brink of love mostly feels jittery. So they are quite apt to try to diminish their jitteriness by either questioning the whole thing, or by trying to determine how sure they can be of a favorable outcome.

Among some people the questioning shows up as a final bout of ambivalence. Their craving for togetherness may get mingled with nostalgic memories of being free to come and go as they please. Consequently just as the momentum is reaching its highest pitch, you may feel them riding the brakes ever so slightly.

This is fairly predictable because under these circumstances their ruminations about your sincerity tend to automatically trigger some form of self-protectiveness. When someone feels that they are about to fall in love, they instinctively brace themselves before they completely give in to it.

More often than not, then, if your partner shows ambivalence at this point it's generally a result of their bracing themselves. Usually such ambivalence is just a defensive posture against the possibility of their being disillusioned. The reason it crops up as ambivalence is because of the overwhelmingly greater desirability of togetherness compared with the alternative of remaining alone. To get these alternatives to balance out in their mind people can't help dressing up the less desirable option and posing it to themselves as something worth considering. Nevertheless, if you proceed seductively, any ambivalence on their part will disappear when the togetherness takes complete hold.

* * *

Another way people try to brace themselves is by creating situations that can test your love. They need a sign that would definitely prove their priority in your life. And usually they won't permit themselves to let go completely until they have found this.

At first these tests can apply to the simplest things, such as whether you arrive on time, whether or not you look at someone else, or if you remember certain things they've told you. These issues can serve to reassure them of your sincerity. Eventually, though, these things seem too trivial to be truly convincing. There is too much at stake without some unmistakable proof of how deeply involved you are.

So following the mythical theme in which a lover must surmount an obstacle to prove just how ardently the beloved is desired, your partner may suddenly impose a challenge that can truly test the depth of your devotion.

Depending on how insecure they feel about taking the plunge this challenge may be unexpected and seem disruptive. To determine if there is a real place for them in your life they may want to see how far you will go in renouncing things that keep your world's separate.

Obviously a great deal is riding on how you respond to these demands. But sometimes a couple's respective commitments can be so different that there may be little room for compromise. One key to solving such difficulties may lie in areas where you can renounce certain things explicitly for their benefit. Any decision that you can make which clearly has them in mind can have a bearing on the proof they are seeking. As long as you show a willingness to make some kind of sacrifice for something both of you want together, other demands probably won't put the relationship in jeopardy.

But also remember, what actually creates these demands is that the ideal side of their identity needs to be recognized and validated. Whatever challenge you may be assigned to surmount will really be a double sided yardstick: on one side it will measure the sincerity of your ardor, while on the other it serves to confirm your appreciation of their ideal qualities. In a sense, then, one aspect of their demand is really a struggle with themselves, a test of their own ultimate value.

This is why your compliance with a specific demand may not be as crucial as the validation that you can meanwhile provide during this sometimes tumultuous phase. From the other's standpoint, what will become part of the new love must secure its place by proving that it is worthy of being taken seriously. So what they really need now is for you to find something superlative about them. They need to know that they've made a major impact.

In short, the self-ideal is the final catalyst to another's love. Accordingly, to complete the strategy we are formulating the next issue we need to address is how to go about validating your partner's self-ideal.

Actually by this point it's likely that you have already validated some aspects of their self-ideal. While they were carrying out certain activities that expressed their sexual or social identity, there were no doubt times when they were living up to ideal standards. At those times they were expressing themselves relative to their self-ideal, more than in terms of the specifically sexual or social aspects of themselves. So if you responded with tellingly seductive affirmations, their self-ideal will have received a certain amount of validation automatically.

Still, everyone possesses certain qualities that constitute a distinct part of their ideal identity. In a given person this involves a mental image of the particular qualities that are most meaningful *to them*. Or, as we also might put it, they are accustomed to envisioning their own self-ideal in specific terms.

So simply telling someone you think they are great may not be germane here. With something as individual as their own idea of living up to ideal standards, that kind of blanket generality has little emotional significance. What counts now is validating the specific qualities that an individual has incorporated in their own ideal self-image. There has to be an overlap in what you compliment and how they actually *conceive themselves* ideally.

Fortunately this is far easier to accomplish than you may have realized. It's very likely that you are already accustomed to making the basic distinction that's required to hit the mark. This involves the way you ordinarily classify other people's attitude toward things like scruples, duty, justice, and the nature of responsibility in general. Naturally you have your own standards, and these influence the judgments you make regarding people's conduct in these matters.

But beyond whatever judgments you may make, such things happen to be the best clue to the basic pattern of any given individual's self-ideal. You probably divide people into those who customarily behave in a roughly conventional way, and those who don't. Now this simple distinction can also tell you an awful lot about the specific qualities that a given individual probably idealizes in themselves.

Since even a rough insight into this aspect of another's identity can be the capstone of a successful seduction, let's look into this further.

CHAPTER EIGHTEEN

IDENTIFYING ANOTHER PERSON'S SELF-IDEAL

T he most important thing to keep in mind when you're trying to validate another's self-ideal is that your compliments have to be about things that person actually idealizes in themselves. Not everything in a person's "best behavior" necessarily reflects their ideal self. With most adults this part of their self-image involves certain specific attributes, rather than everything from head to toe. So you need to have some way to identify those qualities which your partner actually considers part of their ideal identity. The purpose of this chapter is to show you how this can be done.

* * *

Generally speaking, anytime a person expresses intentions that would entail extraordinary efforts you can validate their self-ideal simply by acknowledging that they seem capable of doing whatever it would take to accomplish such intentions. When you regard someone as seeming completely capable of achieving even the most problematical part of their higher aspirations, this expressed belief will tacitly validate that person's self-ideal.

However there is an even more common situation in which this normally hidden aspect of another's identity will be operating. But in order to recognize when, first you must learn which kind of values your prospective lover is truly serious about. Despite the fact that most people today seem to accept any and all lifestyles as being permissible, everyone has certain values that are quite important to them. In fact *some of the values they hold are intimately associated* with the ideal side of their identity.

The kind of values I'm referring to concern your partner's general attitude toward the things we just mentioned, like scruples, duty, justice, and the nature of responsibility. Normally people regard these things in a fairly consistent way. Furthermore, the values related to such things usually have an ideological slant which tends to be either conventional or non-conventional. These divergent attitudes also tend to be linked with either a conservative or liberal outlook.

Of course, anyone's allegiance to either of these ideological orientations is a product of many factors. But the most decisive one usually lies in the congruence that a particular view has with a person's native temperament. One of the pioneers of political psychology, Else Frenkel-Brunswick described this interrelation as "a personalization of the entire social outlook."[1] Stated differently, the values someone characteristically favors generally match their inherent temperament.

The correspondence between these two things can be seen from an early stage in a person's development. In fact most of the research done on this topic has been conducted on school children. It appears that during maturation all children learn that both circumstances and character influence what takes place in life.

And yet the relative importance they attach to either circumstances or character varies substantially among different individuals. It has been found that the ones who came to favor a liberal outlook were those who were temperamentally disposed to resolve stress by looking for the precipitating circumstances. And just as consistently, those who relied on the strength of their character to control stress usually ended up with a conservative outlook.

This corresponds with the fact that people usually have one or another kind of temperament, that is, temperament comes in two notably distinct varieties. On the most fundamental level, a person's temperament reflects how they inherently respond to stress.[2] On one hand some people try to eliminate stress directly, either by controlling, or getting rid of it immediately. For those who deal with stress this way there is a great deal of reliance placed on the strength of their own character.

In marked contrast, other people try to address the *causes* of stress, so as to eliminate it. With them the emphasis is less on their own character, and more on the circumstances which have produced the stress. For these people the solution lies in finding ways to change the circumstances.[3]

Now, in keeping with this divergence we also find *a marked difference in the kind of qualities* that individuals with either type of outlook tend to favor as ideals of personal conduct. The following example will illustrate this: the liberal G. B. Shaw wrote that "a man who is not a revolutionary by twenty is an inferior." On the other side of the aisle Goethe said "The weak often have revolutionary sentiments."

If we look closely at these opposed attitudes they clearly suggest which kind of qualities each orientation tends to idealize. By way of contrast, the way these two eminent thinkers felt about "revolution" tells us that each held certain forms of behavior in high regard. Goethe obviously favored qualities which support established traditions, and so looked unfavorably on revolutionaries. Shaw felt the same way about qualities associated with effecting changes, and therefore regarded revolutionaries as superior.

* * *

Before continuing, perhaps I should explain why this divergence is generally the rule rather than the exception. You know that the values a person holds can influence their actions. Well, this works the other way around just as strongly: a person's characteristic way of acting leads them to regard certain values as being more "right" than others. Though we normally only think about values in terms of their moral wholesomeness, there is also the fact that people often have to implement values in their behavior. So given the conflicts that can arise between values and conduct, most people tend to favor the kind of values which fit in with their native temperament.

And this shows up mostly in certain habits that characterize different people, such as restraint and discipline, or in marked contrast, forbearance and tolerance; one or the other usually fits a given person quite well because it is ultimately a manifestation of that person's temperament. Accordingly, we consistently find that qualities which can be used to support traditional values tend to figure prominently in a conservative's self-ideal. In the same way, qualities connected with finding ways to change things have a central place in how a liberal views themselves ideally.

Here lies the crucial point: since people are more comfortable with their own respective attitude toward responsibility, this also has a strong affect on determining the particular kind of qualities that someone is going to consider as ideal attributes of themselves. For instance, a truly authentic beachcomber probably wouldn't consider job related diligence to be a virtue; nor is it likely for them to adopt such a quality as part of their own self-ideal. Neither would a workaholic view a capacity to just let things be, as being worthy of anyone's applause, especially not his.

This is why attitudes toward the nature of personal responsibility are the best clue to a given individual's self-ideal. When a person expresses either their conservative or liberal values it can key you into the specific qualities that they probably idealize in themselves.

* * *

Since this territory is not customarily considered from a strictly tactical standpoint, let me emphasize that that is our only purpose here. Here again, as with introversion and extroversion, both ways are morally equivalent: neither is better or worse than the other because stress in fact has both immediate and contingent implications. Until utopia arrives it will be necessary for some people to control, and for others to try to resolve the stressors which effect us all alike.

Meanwhile the strategic significance of the distinction being made here begins with your becoming familiar with a person's ideological viewpoint. This will then serve as a clue to the particular qualities which they probably consider as being ideal attributes of themselves (these will be described in the next chapter).

So let me reiterate the basic tactic here. Quite often we find people trying to validate their role as being dedicated, knowledgeable, resourceful, or even witty with respect to their expressed values. Just as often when a person is making that kind of attempt, it could also involve an unconscious desire to validate their self-ideal. Accordingly, your agreement with the values they express can mean a lot to them.

But even more importantly, the general tenor of their values will indicate which specific qualities hold the most intimate significance for a given individual's identity. Once you can put your finger on these specific qualities, and zero your validations in on them, that's it. So restricting a very complex issue to the limited purpose of our discussion, let's pursue this clue into the nature of a person's self-ideal along its two divergent lines.

CHAPTER NINETEEN

VALIDATING YOUR PARTNER'S SELF-IDEAL

PORTRAIT OF A TRADITIONAL SELF-IDEAL

Anyone who usually displays a tendency to confront stress directly will tend to put little stock in chastened, wistful virtues. The only kind of qualities that will appeal to them as ideals of personal conduct will be ones that can serve to directly reduce or control the stress presented by outside pressures.

Using this as a base, we find that one of the specific qualities which a conservative is likely to idealize in themselves is *directness*. This quality is based on an undaunted willingness to face the immediately given manifestations of a problem. Since they tend to be concerned with what is directly creating stress, they celebrate not being easily distracted by indirect causes or ulterior reasons. Or as Goethe put it, "Hoping and waiting is not my way of doing things."

This is also why it is not altogether strange that conservatives are usually willing to apply force in upholding righteousness.[1] And as I indicated before, this puts a premium on *strength*, which often comes through as *directness*.

Another trait that reflects strength is *single-mindedness.* A person strong on the virtue of strength is also strong on having his or her bearings pointed in a definite direction. As Goethe expressed this, "The mind endowed with active powers, and keep(s) ... to the task that lies nearest, is the worthiest on earth."[2]

The point to remember, then, when seeking to validate a conservative's self-ideal is that when they display either directness or single-mindedness, your assent or approval will probably be right on the mark. Seldom are either of these traits expressed merely gratuitously.

* * *

Also associated with "strength" is a wish to personify qualities which connote that he or she can be relied on. So the traits of *trustworthiness* and *dependability* often have a special place in their self-ideal. Accordingly, any show of confidence in their reliability is apt to induce more than a faint acknowledgment. And by this point an overt accolade along these lines may be all that remains for you to reach your goal.

Let's assume that your partner's interest in you has become fairly insistent: at times they think of little else. But for the sake of argument, let's say that the "little else" is enough to hold up their complete surrender. In other words, let's assume that they haven't quite crossed the threshold yet.

As we've seen, quite often this final reservation springs from a lack of assurance that your admiration extends to how they view themselves ideally. Though they've acknowledged that you admire them, they may not be sure whether that admiration includes what they now vaguely sense counts the most.

The sense of imminent surrender also brings questions of fidelity and *trust* into greater focus. When this point is reached, someone with a conservative bent may broach this issue while sharing details about their past. Without sounding sanctimonious, they may describe an occasion when their trustworthiness was put to the test.

Naturally most of their conscious attention will be on how you feel about these things. As Bernard Murstein has pointed out, when a "couple find that they hold similar value orientations in important areas, they are apt to develop much stronger positive feelings for each other ... One reason for this is that when an individual encounters another who holds similar values, he gains support for the conclusion that his own values are correct: his views are given social validation."[3]

This is undoubtedly true. However, when a passionate involvement is about to bloom, something deeper than overt agreement is at stake. So beyond seeing eye to eye on the value of fidelity this is your best opportunity to validate a very personal aspect of a conservative's self-ideal. His or her description of prior instances where their *reliability* was demonstrated is a tacit projection of a cardinal aspect of their self-ideal. So if you make it a point to accord this due appreciation, any remaining reservations on their part should melt away completely. Remember, the apex of love's ascent is always tied in with the apex of a person's identity.

* * *

Another idealized tenet among conservatives is the indispensability of established norms. Such standards are generally embodied in ethical codes. Most conservatives are followers of what has been accepted as being right, and how this applies here and now. In keeping with their acceptance of established ethical codes they generally place a high value on *loyalty*.

Loyalty reflects a person's devotion to something, be it a custom, standard, an organization, or another person. The measure of a person's loyalty lies in how far they can live up to certain obligations. Here again, whenever this quality is displayed your expressed appreciation of it will validate one of your partner's most sensitive self-feelings.

In today's prevailing modernistic atmosphere the quality of loyalty finds few areas that it can routinely be applied to. But it often shows clearly in a conservative's attitude to their friends. Paradoxical as it may appear, conservatives are quite liberal with respect to faults in those close to them. They tend to have faith in their friends and associates and are unwilling to believe ill of them. But rather than just being blind trust this usually reflects their strong sense of loyalty. So be prepared not to be too moralistic if you find reason to judge one of their friends negatively. Instead, applaud his or her loyalty.

There is another way in which established standards carry over to what conservatives typically personify as an ideal self-attribute. This involves codes of interpersonal conduct, particularly with strangers. Displays of politeness, courtesy, and good manners frequently convey more than simply the mark of good breeding. They also represent qualities that are probably enshrined in his or her self-ideal.

Of course we can't compliment such conduct like a parrot each time its displayed. But a conservative's penchant for cultured manners frequently extends beyond what is consistent with routine occasions. For example, they tend to thank people for a service even when it is their job to provide it. Or they may be helpful in little acts without being asked to, as in being thoughtful not to increase someone else's duties.

Here is where a compliment regarding their considerateness can reach well within the ideal region of their selfhood. Any act of thoughtfulness, particularly with respect to a third party deserves a comment like, "That was very considerate of you. You could have created a spectacle that would have embarrassed them," or whatever may be applicable in this respect.

However, the guiding principle to identifying a conservative's self-ideal is not mainly found along these lines. Instead, whether the conservative is male or female, introvert or extrovert, young or not so young, American or Russian, their self-ideal will largely revolve around qualities associated with strength of character. And since it is that kind of quality which they consistently hold up as the most appropriate for themselves, this is what you should keep your eyes pealed for.

* * *

Before proceeding further, let me remind you that our only aim here is to identify the attitudinal traits which are apt to be idealized by a given person. To some extent approaching this in terms of a liberal/conservative dichotomy invites comparisons as to the corresponding merits of either outlook. While talking about the traits of one group, it may seem to imply that those in the other category are deficient in the traits being named. But such an implication would be far off-base.

When generalizing about either orientation's ideal qualities we must remember that everyone ultimately has an individual mixture of qualities in varying proportions. Consequently the importance of any generalization is always relative or approximate. There can always be other factors that are more important in determining a particular person's overall makeup.

Still, when we look at the larger averages certain uniformities are usually clearly evident. Therefore, instead of trying to complete this jigsaw puzzle by throwing half of it away, we can at least use some of the larger pieces as a lead to the whole picture. So continuing with this broad dichotomy let's now examine the qualities compatible with a liberal temperament.

PORTRAIT OF A NONCONVENTIONAL SELF-IDEAL

Because this world is still far from being perfect, those with a liberal outlook find many social conditions open to improvement. They see that circumstances bear down harder on some people than on others. And they recognize that part of this doesn't arise from the nature of things, but from the way mankind has organized society. As a rule they also believe that such things are susceptible to reform through human efforts.

The "reformer's" agenda is therefore quite typical among those disposed to this outlook. Nor is it uncommon for them to become active in various forms of progressive movements. Now these kinds of activities place an emphasis on a capacity for *innovation*. A concern to resolve social problems demands an ability to develop new ways from which to view all existing routines.[4]

True, such matters are not commonly a focal point during private encounters. Still it's likely that sooner or later mention of these interests will be made. Offhand it might seem that the element of altruism implied in such concerns should be singled out for validation. One feature of a liberal's behavior is their willingness to sacrifice themselves for no apparent material or personal gain. This lends an altruistic aura to a reformer's efforts which naturally figures prominently in their pantheon of virtues.

And yet this is seldom the kind of personal trait that someone with a liberal perspective singles out as an ideal in themselves. More commonly the quality that holds an inwardly personal significance is *innovativeness*. It is largely their capacity to find original positions that has the strongest ideal significance for those who fall into this category.[5]

The reformer's agenda generally involves using novel approaches, defining new goals, and devising the means for their realization. Sometimes this is outwardly expressed in what may seem to be utopian pronouncements. Such pronouncements, as even they themselves will admit, are still highly debatable. Nevertheless their greatest pride comes from conceiving of innovations that "could" bring about improvements. So it is in relation to these innovative ideas that your validation can register most profoundly.

* * *

A penchant for reform also presupposes at least a moderate disdain regarding established customs. Outwardly this often lends a nonconventional air to many of the liberal's perspectives. Sometimes this is expressed in actions that may connote an infringement, because as the phrase has it, "certain things go without saying."

To some extent practically everyone becomes the sort of person he or she is by relating to others according to established conventions. To that extent our responses are characteristic of the society in which we were reared. Particularly in the presence of others, these normative conventions set a boundary on what ordinarily transpires between people.

This conventional substratum plays a role in interpersonal cohesion and as a normative source of tact. For many it forms a guiding principle for much of their behavior. Because of this consensual foundation some of us occasionally find ourselves wondering, "What will people think?"

In marked contrast, others routinely exhibit what R. B. Cattell termed a "bohemian unconcernedness."[6] Though this characterization is a bit dated, it catches the flavor of a basic quality generally considered ideal by those who hold innovation in high regard. They like to appear unconcerned with conventions, or what amounts to the same thing, to impress others with startling remarks or unusual behavior.

So it seems hardly surprising that some of them habitually sound off against established codes or prohibitions. A few even use curse words in this vein as if they were audible exclamation points. But more often than not this censoriousness is not intended to be malicious. Underneath it is an attempt to validate a prominent aspect of their unconventional persona.

Here the relevant tactic to keep in mind is that since they too were raised in a consensually ordered reality, it takes a real effort to "be" unconventional. To deliberately decorate what might normally be considered an infringement takes energy. So rather than responding with shock, it is better to act as if you are pleasingly astonished. The effect of responding this way is that it will allow your partner to be proud of themselves, or at least not feel foolish for having made such an effort.

As a rule these people view the fashions of the day with an ironic diffidence. On a personal level, finding their own version of meaningful work, their own concept of beauty, their own interpretation of truth, and approaching these somewhat self- indulgently, are looked upon as being virtues which rank as ideal.

Basically they try to keep their self-image free from conventional criteria. They seem bent on holding no conviction, except that all convictions are questionable. This could be called a blend of independence and skepticism. Acted out in everyday terms, they manifest this by keeping out of step with customs, or at least pretending to do so. Remember, though, that in these instances their line of conduct is not only quite authentic for them, but they also regard such conduct as being superior, and so something suitable to idealize in themselves.

* * *

With those who are not as interested in dealing with social conditions, the significance of being original still remains a basic trait. But among these, their penchant for originality has to be expressed with respect to the more happenstance issues of everyday affairs. Accordingly, many of these individuals become adept at finding all kinds of original connections in what we generally take for granted.

In some cases their need to be innovative is channelled into some sort of artistic expression. But lacking such an outlet a majority apply their taste for originality to making observations on what-have-you, yet observations which often have novel implications. Most people in this mold can readily find symbolical meaning in what we loosely call everyday things.

Another way to describe this trait in those with a unconventional temperament would be as intuition or even insight. They are constantly thinking things out from a new angle, because their intuition continuously suggests fresh possibilities. In fact, sometimes these ideas come so suddenly that they themselves are unable to work out exactly how they came upon them. They may express a strong conviction as to the truth of something apart from any obvious support.

But rather than making this an occasion for debate, this affords you an incomparable opening for validating precisely what they generally consider their cardinal ideal quality. The most rewarding validations come to them when they are not entirely sure whether they are right about something. So if you assert that it does in fact seem true, they are apt to take this more broadly as a validation of what is for them an ideal attribute.

Obviously the significance that your validation can have for someone's self-ideal rests on their accepting this as being genuine. Considering the sketchy evidence that these people often have for their spontaneous insights, this might appear to be difficult in the present connection. But two points should be kept in mind.

First, these intuitive judgments very often prove to be absolutely correct and to the point, when checked by later experience. Owing to their habitual focus on the relation between things, individual's in this mold generally develop a capacity to see what ordinarily goes unnoticed. They have a special flair for grasping the less salient aspect of things, and pointing them out correctly.

Secondly, since most of us don't cultivate this capacity in ourselves, it stands out as being unusual. So it has just the nonconventional air about it that fits in with their predilection for what is off the beaten path.

As it is, there is an invisible line between the ordinary and the extraordinary which keeps what pertains to love separate from what ordinarily prevails in life. So for those who favor the unconventional road, your validations of their different ways will be a tacit guarantee that here at last they have a knowing and accepting, if not kindred, spirit.

* * *

The two portraits we've looked at are rendered in very broad strokes. However, they should be adequate to convey the general nature of the qualities which rank as ideal among those with either of the orientations we've distinguished.

We have seen that there are two noticeably different varieties of personal ideals. And each one gets its respective coloring from the type of values that a particular person is most comfortable with. Therefore the particular qualities which a given person idealizes in themselves can be easily identified by a seducer who knows what he or she should look for.

All you need to do is to look for these qualities as you would the details in the pattern of a tapestry, or the recurrent themes that reappear throughout a piece of music. This is where having a foreknowledge of what ultimately leads to passionate love can help you to validate not only what constitutes the apex of a person's identity, but what is unquestionably the most fertile area in which to generate their deepest passion.

On the other hand, if a meaningful interaction on this level does not occur, and sustenance for the validity of the other's self-ideal is not provided, part of their longing for fulfillment may not be sated. For deep, passionate, romantic love to blossom, a lot depends on whether your partner's ideal self gets to manifest its lineaments, and is welcomed as something worthy of being taken seriously.

CONCLUSION

The love experienced as "being in love" . . . is characterized by simultaneously containing these two ingredients: the feeling of being "enchanted" by another being who produces an encompassing illusion in us and feeling oneself "absorbed" in them down to the roots of our personality as if they had pulled us out of our normal anchorage and we were living with our vital roots transplanted in them . . . What is essential to this romantic species of love is a *combination of the two elements* we mentioned: the *enchantment* and the replanting of our roots so that they are now nourished by the other. This combination is not a mere coexistence, not a matter of their existing side by side, but rather that *each is born and is nurtured by the other*. It is a giving oneself over to being enchanted. (my translation and italics).

JOSE ORTEGA y GASSET,
Estudios Sobre el Amor

CHAPTER TWENTY

DOING IT GOOD

T he foregoing sections have focused on the most predictable factors that can bring virtually anyone to fall in love. Based on several well established premises, we outlined a strategy which ensures that everything needed to have a profound affect on your future lover will be fully provided for. Applying this strategy will kindle the kind of emotional attachment that another person must feel in order for you to unfailingly win their love.

However, our discussion of seduction wouldn't be complete without saying something about how this strategy can be optimally applied. Though your understanding of the underlying motives of love is indispensable to achieving a successful seduction, the manner in which you apply these insights can definitely augment their impact on your partner.

By "manner" I mean your general overall behavior while you are relating to your intended lover. At some early stage this should serve to convey that you possess two particular qualities which will impress your partner as being nothing less than enchanting. What makes the qualities I have in mind so special is their ability to enchant a partner. As we already noted, what enchants people the most is for them to see that your response doesn't spring out of some long standing need within yourself, but is prompted completely by the delight you take in them.

This means that something is required from you which will guarantee that the other gets to form this kind of impression. Optimally it should be something that fits in perfectly with the deep satisfaction you will be instilling in them by using our strategy. Under these conditions they will realize that you are responsible for their good feeling, therefore it's easy to add just the right accent to the way they perceive you.

The surest lure that draws a person to love is making them feel fascinated by occasionally doing things which appear downright charming. Love normally entails what Ortega y Gasset referred to as an element of enchantment. However, this doesn't mean that evoking another's love won't depend primarily on your providing them with the kind of self-satisfaction we have spelled out throughout this book; but in addition to that they also can come to see you as someone who is unmistakeably enchanting, simply because you radiate that you enjoy being with them.

The optimal condition which guarantees that passionate love will emerge involves a combination of two things. First, there is the subjective state which you have to induce in the other's self-feelings. Besides that, there will also be an affect produced by how they come to perceive you objectively. The complete range of feelings that inspire love combines a subjective affect with an affect produced mainly through cognition, that is to say, by the nature of the qualities someone sees in you.

Obviously you possess certain qualities that other people can appreciate to varying degrees. In a given case this would mainly depend on how well your particular qualities happen to match another person's preexisting preferences in these matters. However, that kind of lucky coincidence is not at all what we are going to be concerned with now.

Yes, it is widely believed that people favor certain qualities, and that these play the main role in the choices they make in their love life. (*cf.* Chap. 8) But the reality is that for most people, their established preferences seldom have that much influence over the attachments they actually wind up forming.

This is not to say that your given store of winsome attributes is therefore irrelevant: far from it. But what I'm getting at is that there exist two specific qualities which *always* produce an impression that evokes enchantment. These two particular qualities far outweigh the importance of anyone's preexisting favorite attributes, especially amid the intoxicating atmosphere of an unfolding romance.

More to the point, the nature of the first quality involves a particular form of behavior which reflects that you are *accustomed to enjoying* whatever you pursue for enjoyment's sake. The second quality that can be banked on to inspire enchantment involves your manifesting a *genuine interest* in who and what the other is really like.

Normally the fervor of a dawning romance is enough to bring out these particular charms in all of us. But since we have decided not to rely entirely on fate's dispensations, let's put these two qualities under a microscope so that you will be sure to have a firm grip on them in the future.

211

AN APPETITE FOR PLEASURE

In people's experience with others they are presented with a wide diversity of personalities. Some are sensitive, others serious, others may be profound or pragmatic, plodding or impulsive; or some can be sentimental, others are ambitious, etcetera. Such traits represent the wide divergence found among all of us in our general nature or overall personality.

Generally these things create an impression which is conveyed to those we encounter in romantic contexts. And they invariably influence their subsequent expectations. For instance, if you were to appear sensitive it would suggest that your love will be delicate, or if you appear trustworthy it suggests that you are going to be faithful. These qualities would carry a "recommendation," particularly for anyone who already has a preexisting soft spot for either quality.

But there is a partiality for one particular quality which virtually everyone shares, and the prospect of romance makes them keep an eye out for its presence in you. This particular soft spot stems from the degree of pleasure people have come to expect from love. Since love is the most fulfilling thing that nearly anyone can experience, the most decisive sign that you can provide this for someone else, the quality that counts most, is *how easily you yourself appear to find fulfillment.*

This comes across best through a certain manner which inadvertently reveals just how much we trust ourselves. I'm not referring to confidence, which properly must relate to a specific task, as in being confident about using ice skates. The quality I'm referring to generally manifests itself more subtly in the basic outlook with which we meet life's recurrent, moment to moment situations. But most of all, this particular form of self-trust shows up in the zest with which you approach situations that involve enjoyment.

* * *

The conscious aim of romantic relations largely involves the pursuit of pleasure. Therefore by displaying your capacity and readiness to assimilate enjoyment, it will serve to suggest that the situation which will exist between you and your partner is going to be filled with pleasure. But that isn't all: when someone sees your ability to enjoy various situations it is very likely to stimulate their own appetite to indulge in pleasure.

This tends to happen spontaneously through people's tendency to imitate your positive qualities, particularly the ones they can see will contribute to their own enjoyment. Though imitation is mostly attributed to young children, the tendency to mimic others' conduct stays with everyone throughout life. Therefore imitation can always serve to awaken desires for pleasure, which without concrete examples of their feasibility, your partner might not have started dwelling on yet.

From your partner's standpoint, the measure of how much pleasure they can expect to share with you comes mainly from their finding themselves imitating your assimilation of pleasure. This works with the same regularity that a yawn in one person induces a yawn in another, but in precisely the opposite direction. That is, by being highly imitable, a pleasure seeking mannerism on your part can serve to awaken the other's sometimes drowsy appetite for self-indulgence. When they perceive this quality in you, it will remind them that they too possess it.

Perhaps we can underscore this point by referring to its rueful opposite. Few things are more boring than a bored person. Amid their long silences, we can almost make out the refrain, "I'm not going to sing for my supper." With a few sparse grunts, they seem to demand that one has to amuse them. But it's usually a lost cause because their apathy makes everything ungratifying — for both of you.

Accordingly, whenever possible, your conduct should provide clear evidence that you expect to be gratified, that you expect to derive whatever enjoyment might be gotten from a given situation. When your usual bearing repeatedly radiates this zestful assumption your openness to pleasure will set the tone for what the other can expect from you.

In short, there is no other quality which dovetails quite as perfectly with our strategy of seduction as making your own qualifications as a connoisseur of enjoyment clearly evident. Either through being directly imitated, or by indirectly suggesting that there is something about the other that you enjoy greatly whenever you are with them, this quality is insuperable.

AN AUTHENTIC CURIOSITY

Another quality which regularly generates enchantment involves an unmistakable form of curiosity. This kind of curiosity stands out in that it transcends our normal preoccupation with how things affect us, and fixes completely on how they affect the other.

Whoever you choose to seduce, he or she will be a unique and unduplicatible being. Inasmuch as everyone feels like this it forms one of the most fundamental conditions for the existence of passionate love. We can love several siblings, two parents, and according to Fromm, all of mankind in a brotherly way. But unlike those manifestations of human affection passionate love presupposes an attraction and union between just one me and one very specific you. That is, passionate love is a sublime absorption in one specific individual.

Lovers love each other exclusively: they find one another interesting because of each one's seemingly matchless qualities. This is why another person will be drawn into a magical spell if you show an authentic curiosity to understand who they really are, as well as have been, and want to be. This kind of curiosity is another ineluctable source of enchantment. Your curiosity about how they differ from others, about their specific way of existence, or their particular way of doing things will convey that you are not merely a passing onlooker, but someone taken by something unmistakably compelling.

This is no run-of-the-mill occurrence. When a person gets caught up in your sustained and authentic interest in what they are all about, they will bask in the warmth which this far from common situation radiates. By seeing how much attention their presence stimulates in you, they can't help but feel that what you are beholding in them must be permeated with significance. It will seem that this must appeal enough to you to keep you focused on it. And this is what will make your sustained interest a source of enchantment.

However, to guarantee that enchantment is evoked you must do more than just relate to the other attentively: it has to be unmistakable that your interest is in who that person is in themselves, and not with an eye to how this might be of service to you. So simply observing them continuously won't do. Your curiosity needs to be unbiased enough to lift you above your preconceptions of how people should act. Then you will see not only how, but why they act as they do. And this will allow you to relish both their strong points and understand their weaker ones.

The more your interest in someone uncovers things which you understand, the more this very same interest will draw out those deeper expressions of pride, humility, fear and hope in them which you yourself cherish and respect. So as the other's way of living becomes more intelligible to you, that will automatically keep more of your attention focused on them. And this will assuredly make them feel enchanted with you. Then you can both revel in the good fortune which prodded you to seduce them.

* * *

In the same way that love's underlying motives involve exactly the same aspects of identity in everyone, the two qualities we have just pointed to can be counted on to inspire a decided enchantment with you in practically anyone. This form of shared pleasure and sustained absorption in another individual is the essence of the enigmatic mood which runs through every romance from one end to the other, whether for a brief fling, or for a lifetime.

Your ability to relish pleasure and get most of it from the one you are with, will awaken the other's desire to make transparent everything about them that can add fuel to the flame. Then the passion will deepen when your continued curiosity seems as if it could fathom even what is deepest about them. And the one you behold in this way will want you to seduce them. Yes, over and over and over.

CHAPTER TWENTY ONE

THE FRUITS OF SEDUCTION

T hroughout this book the emphasis was placed on the self-enhancement which your partner is going to get from having the ideal, social, and embodied aspects of their personal identity affirmed. When you do this seductively, it will affect them unconsciously as being a global confirmation of their unconditional worth. At first blush it might seem that this would lead them to become pretty self-absorbed. Actually, though, nothing is as conducive to their *selflessness* as this three dimensional enhancement of their selfhood.

Once the catalytic influence of your seductive affirmations have had their intended affect on your partner's most sensitive self-feelings, that individual's major concern will shift from dwelling mainly on his or her own self to caring just as much about you. Instead of passively indulging themselves in an orgy of self-admiration, he or she will be moved beyond the confines of their own ego, transported by an all consuming desire to be with, or become part of you.

Evolution has shaped the human mind so that in addition to attending to each individual's own self-preservation, it is quite capable of applying itself just as vigorously, and sometimes even more easily, to someone else's well being. This is why once you've

confirmed the substance of your partner's worth, he
or she will no longer only be preoccupied with just
what lies within the boundary of their own ego.

Love has the supreme power to get a person to
transcend their self-absorption, for getting them
out of themselves, and getting them absorbed in
someone else. Love is born when someone long
accustomed to thinking mostly about themselves
starts to think more about the one who has seduced
them. Your seductive dedication will enable them to
care as much, or more, about you as they do about
themselves.

* * *

Fortunately, very fortunately, this also applies
to you. Once you possess the other's love, it won't
only bring you the rich rewards inherent in that —
it will remove the finite boundary around your own
ego too. Then by lifting you out of the everyday
confines of your ego, love will bring you into contact
with your authentic self.

And this is not just a matter of being able to say
what's really in your heart. Authenticity is being
content with yourself just as you are; it comes from
having a reason to accept being nothing more than
what you can be. Everything gets pulled back into
perspective because at any given moment that's
always enough. Few rewards are richer than being
able to be glad that you're yourself.

* * *

But there is more: once you've seduced someone
into loving you, that will also lay the foundation for
an even greater achievement. Any time a love lasts,

it does so because the same conditions which led to its birth continue to affect both participants in exactly the same way. So when you've attained someone's love through your knowledge of what it takes to do this, it remains forever in your power to keep it. The circle can be kept expanding simply by doing what started it all.

Then gradually, as your seductiveness becomes second nature, all trace of effort will be long forgotten. For as the Kama Sutra tells us, ". . . once the wheel of Kama starts to turn, there (are no) rules, only the numbing ecstasy of motion."

All in all, these priceless rewards are what make whatever effort a seduction may initially demand, one of life's most rewarding investments.

APPENDIX

. . . well-known stimuli working under well-known conditions produce well-known reactions.

A. N. WHITEHEAD,
Adventures of Ideas

UNRAVELING THE MYSTERY OF LOVE

C urrently there is a consensus emerging in scientific circles regarding the basic motives of romantic love. Using objective experiments, a number of investigators have arrived at a consistent body of conclusions about this phenomenon. In large part the concept of love used in this book is based on this experimental research.

However, to fashion a truly workable definition of love, it was necessary to also utilize data drawn from philosophy as well as some based on clinical observation. There are certain basic facts which have been uncovered in these two lines of inquiry, that when taken together and synthesized with the experimental findings, define love more thoroughly than today's experimental tradition does by itself. To show that this is the case, this appendix will review each of the traditions out of which our current perspective has been developed. It will follow a chronological sequence that traces the sources from which this book's perspective is derived.

SECTION I
PHILOSOPHICAL ANTICIPATIONS OF
TODAY'S CONCEPT

The history of the concept of love begins with Greek civilization. However, while the glory of ancient Greece is often justly praised, it is also fair to admit that Hellenic civilization lent its prestige to several simplistic ideas which have filtered down through the ages. The somewhat mystical notions many people still have about love are among these.

When the early Greeks began speculating about love they applied an illusory line of thought. As far as they could make out the attraction between two people is ruled by the same cosmic force which allegedly governs all of nature. It seemed to them that this force effects everything from inorganic particles to the motion of the stars. So when this cosmic force enters a person's life, they believed it happens independently of their own motives.

Fortunately, our culture's philosophical traditions also originated about the same time. Accordingly, the idea that love is a metaphysical force was gradually being replaced by philosophical insights into the workings of personal motives.

For example, Plato regarded love as stemming from a deep human craving to enjoy a state of togetherness. Writing metaphorically, he depicted love as a yearning to reestablish a lost unity which had characterized the way of life among man's earliest ancestors. He reasoned that as civilization developed, people had become more separate from each other, thus creating a sense of personal isolation. Evidently Plato felt that a state of togetherness is something indispensable to fulfill man's inherent social nature. By bringing two people together, love provides them the togetherness that had been enjoyed by man's original ancestors.

This somewhat "evolutionary" concept is foreshadowed in Plato's *Timaeus,* and made explicit in the *Symposium.*[1] In the latter Aristophanes declares that the closeness achieved by lovers is the only way in which their yearnings for union can be consummated. Two thousand years later Erich Fromm echoed the same basic idea when he wrote:

> The experience of separateness arouses anxiety: it is, indeed, the source of all anxiety ... The deepest need of man, then, is the need to overcome his separateness, to leave the prison of his aloneness . . . love makes him overcome the sense of isolation and separateness ... In love the paradox occurs that two beings become one and yet remain two.[2]

Despite the centuries separating them both the philosopher and the psychologist saw the yearning for love as a search to transcend one's personal isolation, or as Plato called it, to find one's "other half." The sense of oneness bestowed by a loving union continues to be a prominent theme in theories of love. But now this is seen as only one piece of the puzzle which makes up the complete picture.

* * *

Another philosopher whose views also contributed to current thinking is Rene Descartes. He was the first to see that love is stimulated simply by the difference between the sexes. With this he did not mean sex in an erotic sense, but rather in regard to its psychological bearing on a person's gender identity. Referring specifically to the passionate variety of love which had become popular by his time, Descartes wrote:

> It is true that there are various sorts of delight
> ... But the principle one is that which proceeds
> from the perfections which we imagine in a
> person whom we think may become another
> self; for with the difference of sex which nature
> has placed in man, as in the animals without
> reason, it has also placed *certain impressions
> in the brain* which bring it to pass that at a
> certain age, and in a certain time, they
> consider themselves defective, and as though
> they were but the half of a whole of which *an
> individual of the opposite sex* should be the
> other half ... the acquisition of this half is ..
> . represented by nature as the greatest of all
> imaginable goods ... and this inclination ...
> usually receives the name of love.[3] (my italics)

The "impressions in the brain" which Descartes was alluding to, impressions that can make either men or women "consider themselves defective" until someone of the opposite sex becomes their other half is an unmistakable reference to what we now call our "gender identity." For Descartes the personal confirmation derived from winning over a member of the opposite sex stood out as a basic motive for passionate love. In our terms this confirmation simply represents the validation someone of the opposite sex can provide for our own sense of gender identity.

This elementary process may seem quite obvious, yet it took more than three hundred years before it was included in a formal theory of love. In 1969, Richard Centers, professor of psychology at the University of California, objectively established that a need to maintain and enhance one's sexual identity is a primary motive in sexual attraction and love. More graphically, in Centers' own words:

> For a female to accomplish sexual identity and role maintenance and enhancement, requires that the man (conduct himself so as to) allow her to function in her particular variant of the . . . female role . . . experiencing gratification of (this) drive with a particular member of the opposite sex creates strong bonds of attraction and love for him . . .[4]

Perhaps "gender identity" remained such an ill-defined aspect of love for so long because of its very obviousness. But often what is most obvious turns out to be what is most fundamental. In any case, this simple fact remained a mystery until Centers objectively established that the enhancement of sexual identity plays a prominent role in producing romantic attraction.

* * *

Approaching the modern period Henri Beyle (better known as Stendahl) introduced another consideration which continues to influence current thinking on this topic. In his *De l'amour*, Stendahl defined love as an act of imagination in which we magnify the qualities perceived in the other.

Through this process we endow another person with all sorts of perfections. But he explained this in terms of the affect it ends up having on oneself; supposedly by blowing someone up in our imagination it not only raises their significance, but it also increases how much pleasure we get from them. Stendahl termed this process "Crystallization." To some extent crystallization defines the psychological process which gives rise to the mutual idealization that is so common among lovers.

However, Stendahl did not go on to explore the profound affect that this act of imagination has on the person who is being idealized. It remained for Theodor Reik writing nearly two hundred years later to point out that by idealizing someone we hold up a mirror in which they find reflected an image of the person they would like to be. Therefore, the process of "Crystallization" always has an affect on the other person's ideal self-image.

Let me explain this. Stendahl correctly noted that love involves a strong input from the imagination. According to him the essence of the process which leads to love lies in our tendency to idealize a partner whenever we dwell on them. However, in attempting to explain why this happens Stendahl did not grasp the underlying motive behind this quite common form of perceptual bias.

Since the unconscious and its dynamics was not yet understood in his day, Stendahl could only appeal to the operation of a hedonistic principle; this had been used for centuries to explain just about every form of behavior. Here is how he used it to explain the workings of crystallization:

I call crystallization the operation of the mind which, from everything which is presented to it, draws the conclusion that there are new perfections in the object of its love . . . *it springs from the conviction that the pleasures of love increase* with the perfections of its object.[5] (my italics)

According to this, crystallization is based on the heightened pleasure we will get from someone if we endow them with all sorts of perfections first. By making them out to be perfect, we magnify the enjoyment we will receive in relating to them. It's as if we were to add salt to peanuts, to bring out their full flavor. In one sense this rationale does have some validity. On a conscious level the more highly we idealize someone, the more value we can attach to whatever approval we subsequently get from them.

However on the unconscious plane, the underlying dynamics of love actually involve something other than tallying up how much pleasure we expect to get from someone. The really critical issue is not the status of the person who brings us pleasure; what leads to love rests largely on whether another individual can enhance our own sense of unconditional significance. And this involves several aspects of our own sense of self-identity.

So it's not the other's status that triggers love: before we put anyone on a pedestal, they have to have an impact on what makes up our sense of identity first. Beneath the surface love is never determined solely by how highly one person idealizes another. What really matters is whether the particular areas of a given individual's personality which can serve as sources of pleasure are related to their sense of self.

Looked at from our own perspective what is really crucial is not how extravagantly we are idealized, but rather, *in what respect.* If, let's say, my self-ideal includes an infrequently applied ability to drive race cars and the woman I'm interested in comments on my adroitness in driving through city traffic, this will strike a response chord deep within my psyche. However my first conscious reaction would probably be to magnify her perceptive qualities. These would come to be seen as truly remarkable.

In other words, what usually makes us magnify a partner's qualities is the quickening anticipation that our own higher capabilities will soon come to be appreciated. What renders us likely to see remarkable qualities in our partner where others would probably see nothing special, *is that the unconscious drift of our thought has already veered toward our own self-ideal.* Admittedly, this is not how we are apt to view the origin of this idealizing of another. But it is how the unconscious mind invariably responds in contexts which present this sort of subtle opportunity.

* * *

Even though the foregoing three views differ on fundamentals, with Plato placing the emphasis on togetherness, Descartes on gender, and Stendahl indirectly on the self-ideal, each view in fact has an element of validity. As it turned out these three themes would lead to a solution of the mystery behind love's inherent motives. Let me also point out that this did not happen because one of the views proved more correct or important than the others, but rather, through the combined effect of their co-mingling.

Yet despite the breadth of significance that love has in human experience, it never occurred to these thinkers that the wide significance might spring from an equally diverse foundation. So the presupposition that love is a single, undivided entity continued to go unchallenged. As time passed the philosophical development of the concept of love led mostly to disagreement and controversy. Consequently there was never an orderly accumulation or synthesis of those observations which had in fact been valid.

Rather than seeking collective agreement each philosopher devoted most of his energies to expounding the moral implications of his particular view. In this way the philosophical discussion of love became largely a story of contending moral viewpoints. Perhaps this lack of agreement is why their ideas seldom had much influence on the masses.

When the topic of love began to find a wide reading at the beginning of the eighteenth century it was in the works of literary writers. However, though we find varied allusions to love's subjective meaning in the fictions of literature, as we pursue the story line there are no answers, only more questions to ask ourselves. In literature one may find rich descriptions of love's vicissitudes but never an explanation of its essential nature. So despite the reams of romantic literature that has poured out during the last two centuries, love largely retained its mysterious and mythical characterization.

SECTION II
THE ORIGINS OF A
SCIENTIFIC PERSPECTIVE

Sigmund Freud was the first to discover how human passions actually act as a vehicle for love. He discovered that as with many other conscious activities, love ultimately grows out of certain unconscious emotions. Though he eventually overemphasized the influence of a single, sexual motive, his discoveries nonetheless paved the way to our deepened current understanding.

In Freud's early research he had set out to find what causes neurosis. This work convinced him that neurotic symptoms result from a conflict between the conscious ego and certain unconscious desires which also exist within a person. Though unrecognized by the person, the latter desires can strongly affect their behavior. But because Freud's patients had been socialized in the sexually repressive atmosphere of their Victorian society the unconscious desires he identified, repeatedly turned out to be sexual in nature.

Still, by diligently tracing the permutations of these "libidinal desires," Freud discovered more about how the human psyche works than anyone before or since. Such things as projection, sublimation, fantasy formation, and symbolization, were demonstrated to be responses which arise through the interplay of unconscious urges and the conscious ego.

However Freud was led to believe that love is nothing more than one of these secondarily derived processes. As he finally came to view it love is not something independent, but develops largely out of a conflict of the sexual impulse during early childhood. Freud had not been the first to see a direct connection between sex and love, but the analysis of his patients persuaded him that the latter results entirely from the former.

Because of Freud's repeated exposure to repressed sexual urges he wound up defining romantic love as a form of "aim inhibited sex." By this he meant that the "higher and finer" manifestations of love are an indirect and disguised expression of the sexual impulse. In his words:

> ... if the sensual impulsions are more or less effectively repressed or set aside, (which was the rule in Freud's day) the illusion is produced that the object has come to be sensually loved on account of its spiritual merits, whereas on the contrary the merits may really only have been lent to it by its sensual charms.[6]

As Freud saw it the sex drive doesn't evaporate into thin air when it can not be directly expressed. Instead, by being forbidden its demand for relief and satisfaction builds a ground-swell that winds up coming out in the form of romantic thoughts and feelings. While there is certainly an element of truth in this view it is far from being the whole story. As Theodor Reik later objected:

> What Freud called sex in the enlarged sense is an alloy of metals of very differing natures and values ... The situation can be compared with that of a chemist who for a long time

thought a certain substance to be homogenous until a new examination showed this not to be so. The substance turned out to be a ... fusion of very dissimilar components.[7]

Nevertheless, despite Freud's exaggeration of a single motive his penetrating genius opened the door to a real understanding of how love operates in human experience. By demonstrating that the ego is not always conscious of its own motives he showed that much of what transpires in love is governed by forces which usually lie beneath the surface.

* * *

It is no exaggeration to say that we can be aware, vaguely aware, or completely unaware of the motives behind our behavior. But this doesn't mean that we are going to feel like a robot when we're acting out what may be an unconscious motive. As far as we're concerned there is always a good explanation for our behavior and its generally right on the tip of our lips.

Now this is precisely what happens when it comes to love. For instance, after a man has been dating for a while he will recognize that he enjoys himself with a particular woman, that he feels comfortable with her, that he can act naturally, and so on. But as a rule he will not be aware of the specific psychological motives within himself which happen to be producing this reaction. He will only be aware of his perceptions of, and interaction with the other person.

In this type of situation there are usually factors operating that are not obvious to those undergoing the experience. Amid the usual ebb and flow of a personal interaction we seldom focus directly on how things may impinge on our sense of self. That is, there are countless issues which normally hold our attention off of what may in fact be the real issue of the interaction. Therefore unless we are deliberately analyzing our own or another's behavior we probably will not notice what the underlying motives are.

By showing that we can relate to someone without being fully conscious of our motives Freud set the stage for a scientific approach to unravelling the mystery of love. His discoveries made it clear that in order to identify the actual motives behind love it would require the use of experimental means to determine exactly what these motives are.

* * *

The first social scientists to use this approach were sociologists. During the great depression there had been an alarming rise in the divorce rate. Consequently a number of sociologists began studying issues connected with "marriage" and "the family." At first they did not tackle the issue of love directly. For the most part they only focused on the issues of "mate selection" and "marital adjustment." But as these studies progressed, it became increasingly apparent that objective methods could also be applied to even the most intimate topics.

This came through dramatically in 1948, when Robert F. Winch, a young sociology professor, set out to objectively test a theory of mate selection which he had been developing for several years. He referred to this as the theory of "complementary needs in mate selection."

The basic idea behind Winch's theory is that when two people have needs that match up in a complimentary way, they usually become attracted to one another. According to this theory people fall in love when the traits of one partner ideally fit those of the other, the way a key fits a lock. Winch regarded this kind of harmonious intermeshing of needs as "casting the most light on love as it is experienced in our society."[8]

To fully test his hypothesis Winch embarked on a study that took nearly eight years to complete. Initially the study was funded by a grant from North Western University. But due to its extended nature the National Institute of Mental Health later provided additional funding.

First Winch and four other sociologists spent more than a year designing a set of questions that could serve to objectively establish the underlying motives for a person's choice of a mate. The questions were structured so that the relative strength of a person's needs could be ascertained from their answers. In turn, this could be used to compare how well a given person's needs dovetailed with those of their partner.

After combing through the literature on motivation a list of twelve needs and three general tendencies that are fairly representative of the average person was drawn up. For example, the list contained the following needs: that for "Recognition," to spark the admiration and approval of others; the need to be "Deferent," to admire and praise another person; the need for "Dominance," to influence and control the behavior of others; the need for "Abasement," to accept or invite blame or criticism; the need to be "Nurturant," to give sympathy and aid to a weak, helpless or dejected person; the need for "Succorance," to be helped by a sympathetic person or to be indulged.

As you can see, such needs can pair off fairly well if they were to match appropriately in any two given individuals. For instance, someone with a strong need for dominance would probably be attracted to a person who has an equally marked need to be deferent.

By 1950, Winch was ready to put his hypothesis to a scientific test. Working with his associates Winch set up in-depth interviews with 25 couples. The couples selected for the study had all been married under two years so all of them still had a clear recollection of the conditions under which they had chosen one another.

Over the following five months each participant was interviewed for a total of about five hours. This provided the researchers with a file on each individual that ran anywhere from seventy to two hundred pages.

During the next two years each person's file was painstakingly analyzed in order to get an accurate measure of their dominant needs. This was accomplished by making six independent estimates of each individual's needs. Then by comparing these separate estimates with one another, the relative strength of each need was given a numerical value by averaging all the estimates.

Once this had been done with all fifty people, it was possible to use mathematical equations to determine whether or not each person in fact displayed a complimentary meshing of needs with their respective partner. Morton Hunt, writing in a 1959 issue of *Readers Digest* describes what happened next:

> Anyone could see the correlations but only statistical computation could show whether the correlations (in each couple) were large enough to be (objectively) meaningful . . . The ultimate test . . . consisted of taking a reckoning of the whole sample of correlations and measuring what proportion of them favored the theory and what proportion went against it. Winch's group used mathematical methods on a total of 388 pairs of traits: in the end 256 of them showed correlations favoring his theory . . . put another way, Winch's imperfect result is 99.9 per cent proof that the theory of complimentary needs is correct.[9]

Or more succinctly, as a reviewer in the *American Journal of Sociology* put it, "The idea (of complimentary needs) is not new; indeed it is very old, but Winch is the first person to prove that it is true."[10]

* * *

Though Winch's study had focused mainly on the motives underlying mate selection rather than on those directly responsible for the birth of love, his results did have a decisive bearing on this question. First, the findings demonstrated that a number of needs which belong to each individual are what motivate the relationship leading to marriage. Although a partner's needs normally tend to become as important as one's own, Winch's research showed that love is originally formed out of motives that exist within each person's own psyche.

Before Winch's findings were published a number of writers, including Ortega y Gasset and Erich Fromm, had defined romantic love as being essentially altruistic, even in its inception. They alleged that romantic love is founded on a selfless wish to give, or to take care of a beloved. Winch's study flatly contradicts that definition (at least with respect to the specifically romantic form of love we are concerned with here). As Hunt further pointed out, "According to Winch's evidence, the love of man for woman and woman for man is basically self-serving, and perhaps plain selfish. Its primary purpose is to benefit the lover, not his beloved."[11]

Let me hastily add that this conclusion applies only to the genesis of romantic love. It does not apply to certain other manifestations of human love which are essentially selfless.[12] Recently some researchers have alleged that all forms of love have the same basis as that indicated above. For instance, Arthur and Elaine Aron write that, "To love for our own self-expansion seems to be the universal reason for all kinds of love . . . even saints serve others and do penance to God out of a desire to save their own souls."[13] Not only is this a flawed equation of penance with "service," but it totally misinterprets every other version of selfless love, from motherhood to caring for a sick pet that one loves. So without misrepresenting the facts by stretching them further than what they are based on, all we can say is that "self-expansion" is the universal catalyst to romantic love — period!

* * *

Another important implication of Winch's study concerns the fundamental structure of romantic love. His results made it unmistakably clear that this form of love is structured around a number of distinct needs. This stands out because the couples all mentioned that "being in love" had been a precondition to their getting married. Since the findings disclosed that what had originally brought each couple together involved separate needs, their falling in love was obviously also contingent on the operation of several distinct needs. This is to say, the study showed that it was a combination of specific needs, which in being met, had initially prompted each couple to fall in love.

While the needs were being measured during the study the emphasis had been on each one as an independent factor. But in real life these factors are experienced together in an ongoing relationship. This clearly indicates that instead of being some single unitary phenomenon, love actually represents a composite mental state, that is, it stems from a combination, or blending of different needs.

While Winch was the first to objectively prove that romantic relations involve gratifying a number of separate personality needs, the idea that love consists of independent elements had originally been suggested nearly a hundred years earlier by the English philosopher, Herbert Spencer. In his *Principles of Psychology*, Spencer stated that the physical impulse of sex serves as the nucleus for the "composite" state referred to as love. As he put this:

Round the physical feeling forming the nucleus of the whole there are gathered the feelings produced by personal beauty, that constituting simple attachment, those of reverence, of love of approbation, of self-esteem, of property, of love of freedom, of sympathy. All these, each excited in the highest degree and severally tending to reflect their excitement on each other, form the composite psychical state which we call love.[14]

Spencer goes on to explain that by joining these diverse feelings, love "fuses into an immense aggregation nearly all the elementary excitations of which we are capable; and from this results its irresistible power."[15] Though Spencer's list included nine separate elements which involved some overly hair splitting distinctions, his basic idea that love is made up of separate components has been confirmed not only by Winch, but also by a number of other modern researchers.

However, Spencer had concluded that love is a "composite mental state," solely by using inductive reasoning. So with the rise of experimental science at the turn of the century, and the discrediting of philosophy as mere speculation, his idea was largely forgotten. But most good ideas, unlike old soldiers, don't simply fade away: they remain in some dusty volume, waiting to be rediscovered.

UNCOVERING LOVE'S INGREDIENTS

By the middle of the 1960's, most of the research dealing with love was being carried out by social psychologists. As I mentioned earlier this work served to reveal the underlying structure of love. By applying the same experimental methods that physicists use to analyze the structure of matter to issues involving love, the social psychologists found that love is generally so complex because it involves several distinguishable components. Very briefly, here's how this happened.

As experimental studies spread to various universities a number of the researchers' attention was drawn to a similar problem. This involved the fact that those who served as subjects in their experiments often had differing assumptions about what love is supposed to be. While setting up experiments to analyze love it became apparent that people don't all define it in just one way. In addition to this divergence in people's definition of love the researchers had already observed that love usually undergoes changes over time. Increasingly, then, during the early 70's, these multifaceted characteristics of love began to pose a central theoretical issue demanding an explanation.

As often happens with scientific questions, several psychologists working independently from each other all reached a remarkably similar conclusion. The most straightforward way to account for the variances observed in the laboratory was to hypothesize that love itself combines several different components. Given that love expresses itself in differing manifestations, this clearly indicated that it involves several distinct ingredients.

This conclusion not only explains why people would hold varying assumptions, but it also accounts for the changes love undergoes over time.

More specifically, the meaning love has for a given person reflects the priority which a particular component has for that person at a given time. Similarly, the changing emphasis undergone over time is caused by the rising and falling intensity of each component as it comes to primacy and is then succeeded by another one.[16]

After nearly a century Spencer's concept that love is a "composite psychic state" reappeared, only this time completely as a result of scientific observation. And because the social psychologists had mainly focused on the conditions surrounding love's emergence they found that this can be accounted for with far fewer variables than the nine used by Spencer, or Winch's fifteen.

During the past two decades at least a half dozen major theories of love have been put forward which all define it as consisting of three basic components. (See table below.) This agreement on the number of components is truly remarkable, given the fact that each theory was developed separately by researchers using different data bases.

Recent Conceptions of Love's Three Components[17]

Rubin 1973	physical need	attachment	caring
Centers 1975 (amended)	sex & sexual identity	affiliation & interpersonal security	self-esteem
Wilson 1981	sex	attachment	parental tenderness
Gaylin 1986	sexual passion	capacity for fusion	caring
Sternberg 1988	passion	intimacy	commitment
Shaver *et al*, 1989	sexuality	attachment	care giving

As you can see on this table, all the researchers listed agree that there are three components to love. They also agree on the composition of the first two, which have a "sexual" and a "social" aspect to them. However, with respect to the third component there is less agreement, and with good reason because what most of the researchers have done with this one is questionable. That is, they have stretched their definitions in a way that includes loving deeds, *e.g.*, care giving, tenderness, or making a commitment. Only Centers' designation of "self-esteem" as the third component refers to a factor which actually *causes* love. He alone avoids confusing what are preconditions to love with actions which normally only occur once that state has come into being.[18]

This is quite important because deeds such as making a commitment normally only occur after a person has *already* fallen in love. What moves a person to be caring, or enables them to make a commitment presupposes that love already exists.

Now since caring and commitment are not instrumental in love's birth, this means that we have a gap to fill. From both a practical and theoretical point of view, we need to find the third relevant factor which is actually instrumental in love's emergence.

Luckily we don't need to look very far. In the real world anyone falling in love is unconsciously striving to gratify certain basic aspects of their personality. The sexual and social needs listed on the above table represent such aspects of personality. In addition, as Stendahl's observations on mutual idealization showed, a person's self-ideal also plays a prominent role in the birth of love. Therefore, any realistic definition of love must include this intimate aspect of identity.

Altogether, then, this gives us three components, namely an erotically tinged sex-identity need, a social inclusion need, and a need for self-esteem which is largely mediated by a person's self-ideal. Love is cleaved from these three facets of an individual's identity, so they are what a definition of love must encompass. But since the self-ideal was not included in the theories we reviewed, I have devoted the following section to showing why the ideal aspect of identity constitutes love's third component.

SECTION III
THE SELF-IDEAL: FACT OR ILLUSION

Before anything as intangible as the ideal aspect of personality can be included in a definition of love, there is one issue that needs to be clarified. Is the self-ideal, as is so often alleged, just a residue of adolescent fantasy, or does it have a legitimate status in an adult's consciousness of self?

As it is, some readers may question the validity of a concept that refers to qualities which may appear to exist mostly in people's imagination. However there is a good chance that this skeptical view is based on a mistaken view regarding the self-ideal, and the role it plays in love. This involves a very widespread misconception which views these exalted self-representations as not being realistic or even legitimate. In order to confidently include the ideal aspect of personality in a theory of love we must first resolve this question.

As to how it got started, this ill-conceived interpretation came about because the self-ideal has been studied mainly by theorists with a background in psychiatry, that is, in abnormal behavior. According to the clinical perspective, regarding oneself in an idealized way represents an illusory compensation for feelings of worthlessness. The implication is that the self-ideal's role in love is mostly illusory.

This is why the self-ideal has gotten a "bad press" whenever it is mentioned in connection with love. As one recent proponent of this view, T. Blau puts it, "For the love experience to develop, it is necessary that the ego ideal be questioned, not believed, by the individual experiencing the Love Effect . . . One wants to be a certain thing, but one believes that the capability doesn't really exist."[19]

Now if we were to accept this clinically founded (and bounded) view, then the self-ideal should properly be excluded from a theory of love. Reinforcing or validating anyone's self-ideal would ultimately amount to a form of hypocrisy. This would provide them with, as Blau goes on to describe it, an "unreality support."[20] Let us therefore sort out whether the self-ideal is something that is a neurotic aberration, or something which deserves to be taken seriously.

DISTINGUISHING THE NORMAL FROM THE PATHOLOGICAL

The notion that validating another's self-ideal involves reinforcing their illusions is not based on a representative sampling of people in love. It was derived almost exclusively from statements made by individuals undergoing psychotherapy. These were people with emotional problems who were straining to recall long forgotten difficulties which they ostensibly underwent as children. It is from such contexts that we have gotten the inverted formulation which alleges that the self-ideal is a self-deluding fiction.

This basically negative interpretation of the self-ideal's role in love was first popularized by Theodor Reik. As we saw earlier he was the first of Freud's associates to insist that love is based on more than just the sex drive. But Reik continued the older psychoanalytical practice of making generalizations alleged to hold for everyone, on the basis of observations confined mostly to his patients.

So though Reik correctly noted that love is based on certain ego drives, he viewed these mainly from a pathological perspective. Consequently it was never a straightforwardly healthy ego drive that Reik had in mind when he referred to the self-ideal's role in love. Rather, as he expressed it, ". . . love is really a second best, a compensatory way for not obtaining the ego-ideal state."[21]

In Reik's view people fall in love when they think that someone else possesses certain qualities. But these are not just any old qualities. They are ones, Reik tells us, which we envy because they are the particular ones which we have longed to attain ourselves, but know that we are incapable of ever doing so.

By viewing the other as endowed with just those pearls of character which we have supposedly given up on in ourselves, we allegedly derive a sort of indirect gratification in being liked by that person.

As Reik put this:

> As we realize unconsciously that we are full of shortcomings and failures, we nourish a kind of dissatisfaction with ourselves which moves us to search for this ego-ideal outside ourselves. Thus psychologically prepared, we find a person who seems to have all of the excellent qualities we sadly lack and who is, in contrast to ourselves, apparently self-sufficient and self-satisfied . . . The ego which cannot find realization of high demands in itself searches for their fulfillment in another person who now becomes the personification of one's ideal.[22]
> This state is not always conscious, but the person who will find salvation in love is tired, often sick, of himself . . . 'I do not like being Joe' said a patient just before he fell in love... In all cases I could see the origin of the discomfort was dissatisfaction with oneself...[23]

Reik's basic error was that he went on to apply his clinical observations to people who have not been emotionally traumatized. He mistakenly regarded the adulation which the average person confers on another as somehow implying that they too have a low regard for themselves. The obvious fallacy here lies in applying this interpretation universally. But think about this for a moment: If no one in the world has anything that can legitimately be represented as a self-ideal, then there would never be anyone who the rest of us could really envy or identify with.

Considering the emotionally depleted status of the patients with whom Reik was working, a sense of unworthiness was no doubt common among them. However to base a universal account of the self-ideal's role in love, which supposedly includes everyone, solely on the ill-fated experiences of a few emotionally troubled individuals is insidiously false.

* * *

When we look outside the covers of psychopathology books we find that most people are generally not riddled with neurotic self-dislike, nor out seeking illusory compensations. Of course no one can deny the existence or importance of the pathological processes Reik was describing. However the application he made of these processes regarding the motivation of love in the average person is stretching things a bit.

With individuals whose emotions have not been severely traumatized the self-ideal represents a symbol of latent capacities, which lacking favorable conditions, may not yet have been actualized. But a failure to actualize one's ego ideal is something that a normal individual hopes to redress; the ideal can represent a desire that may eventually be achieved.

Basically, what is operative behind most people's self-ideal is a persisting desire to perform competently, using whatever capacities they feel they possess. So while it is not at all rare for a host of circumstantial imperatives to keep people from actualizing all of their capacities, this does not mean that they don't have any, or that they've lost all touch with them.

The point is that some definable capacity usually underlies a person's self-ideal: the image embodies a consciousness of their potential perfectibility. Thus a sense of one's potential best-self is not an empty dream but parallels potentials that might some day be actualized.

* * *

I submit that most individual's self-identity includes a roughly accurate assessment of their own indwelling potential. This is the raw material from which the self-ideal is formed: the idealized image is based on a self evaluation that takes account of the person's own latent potential. And while these potentials are not always apparent, there is a good reason why we can assume that most members of our species do in fact possess them.

Simply by virtue of being a living representative of the human species everyone possess an inborn spectrum of potentials unparalleled in any other organism. However, it is not the least bit unusual for some of this potential to remain unactualized among many of us. Since what we have to shoulder in the flux of our everyday circumstances and responsibilities is what structures our destiny, this can keep us from cultivating everything we might otherwise get to work on. Just the same, for those who are not overwhelmed by a sense of helplessness the indwelling potential serves as the raw material used in constructing their self-ideal.

In order to fully appreciate the implications of this claim, and so the justification for viewing the self-ideal as a normal part of the love experience, it is necessary to consider certain evolutionary facts.

First we need to see that virtually every individual has an inescapable share of biologically given resources, which in the nature of things have no outlet other than through symbolical representations. Then we will be in a position to assess this matter more accurately. Again, to reach this vantage point we must take a broader view of human nature than that available from the analyst's couch.

THE EVOLUTION OF MANKIND'S LATENT POTENTIAL

Every individual alive right now was born with a range of potentials which are just as much an innate part of them as the rest of their physical organism. This biological inheritance comprises the most formidable repertoire of behavioral aptitudes possessed by any known species. You, and virtually every romantic prospect you're apt to choose has a natively given range of behavioral potentials which were created in the slow motion assembly line of evolution.

No one needs an aristocratic lineage to possess these potentials: they are an inherent property of what makes all of us members of our species, that is, these behavioral potentials are contained in the human genotype.[24] The potentials were bequeathed to us by our earliest human ancestors. By successfully adapting to the demanding living conditions of nearly a million years ago, ancient man gradually acquired a range of behavioral potentials whose possibilities still remain inexhaustible.

But since we live in a radically transformed environment, many of the capacities which became part of man's native endowment no longer have to be exercised. That's why these potentials are not always apparent. Because any potential requires appropriate conditions to be drawn out, the absence of such conditions makes it difficult to appreciate that it even exists. To a large extent this is the case with respect to many of the behavioral capacities acquired by the earliest ancestors of our species.

Here you may well ask, what grounds do we have for assuming that these so-called potentials are still part of everyone's native endowment? Offhand it would appear that each person must undergo specific learning to develop potential.

Actually, though, that is an overly simplified view. To be sure, developing a potential into an appliable aptitude certainly does entail a great deal of learning. For instance, to become a concert pianist takes at least ten years of constant practice according to one account. However the inherent dexterity of the pianist's hands is a potential bequeathed by our simian ancestry when they evolved an adaptation to living in trees.

Stated differently, the behavioral repertoire we are talking about is based on response patterns wired into the human central nervous system and brain. They were acquired as successful adaptations to life in a state of nature, and constitute a range of capacities fit to master challenges we can barely imagine.

In order to survive in a state of nature our forebears needed a broad range of skills to gain ascendancy over competing species who are much stronger, deadlier, and who reproduce at a quicker rate. Obviously our presence here today attests to the fact that they in fact acquired such skills: our species would not have survived if they hadn't.

Now when we also recognize that for several hundred thousand years the range of behavior made possible by these skills could only be passed on from one generation to another through genetic inheritance, it becomes apparent that these capacities are part of man's inborn endowment.

But how can we be sure of this? Simply because for several hundred thousand years before civilization came into being, language had not yet evolved. According to the best current estimate language originated roughly 80,000 years ago.[25] Therefore, since language did not exist during more than ninety percent of man's presence on this planet, the behavioral wherewithal required for survival had to be gradually acquired as innate response patterns which could be passed on through genetic inheritance.

Generally most people have been taught to look at the issue of man's ascent as something made possible by cultural indoctrination, rather than as a product of heritable capacities. Properly enough this is the view portrayed in our histories of civilization. From this perspective man's dominant place in nature was won by our culture's ability to pass on organized technologies.

However that is a fundamentally narrow perspective. The fact is that all of man's historical enterprises were originally made possible by the evolutionary struggle which produced the human brain. All the major human attributes, including brain size, intuition, reason, foresight, and intelligence, evolved long before cultural evolution became the dominant medium of man's ascent.[26]

In other words, the human brain did not grow to
its present size merely by accident. To a large
extent its size parallels the range of capacities that
were acquired through natural selection.[27] These
capacities have been wired into the perceptual and
behavioral neural circuits which form the functional substrate of our brains. And as such they
constitute a range of potential still inherited by all
of us.

SOCIALIZATION AND LATENT POTENTIAL

Taken to its logical conclusion, to actualize this
wide spectrum of inherited resources would require
environmental conditions broad enough to fully accommodate all of them. But as you might well
imagine that would necessitate social conditions
verging on a utopia. Unfortunately, though, such
perfect conditions are still a long way off.

So today when that potential is embodied in each
new birth, it has to be sculpted down to match the
dimensions called for in the operations of one's
particular society. What has happened is that with
the standardization of work which has occurred
during the past few centuries, the innate capacities
the average person gets to employ have had to be
increasingly delineated to conform with fixed standards. Put another way, the standardization of
work has cut us off from some of our inborn resources.

Of course in a very unalterable sense this is
scarcely avoidable, given that the reality we must
work with is how it is. Ultimately human existence
could not have unfolded other than the way it did;

therefore a measure of specialized discipline is the only road to adaptation.

Yet in adapting to our civilization we inevitably get separated from the full range of all our inborn capacities, even though we are born with all of them. Given the routinized arrangement of our manmade environmental conditions a significant part of our innate behavioral repertoire automatically remains dormant. In sum, the relation of potential to actualization has become discontinuous, leaving much of the potential irrelevant or unengaged.

The best known example of the tremendous scope which unenacted human potential can take is the destiny allotted to the female sex, from the beginning of patriarchal societies to just the past few decades. The limited activities permitted females throughout recorded history has squandered what must have been an incalculable range of human capacities.

But it is not just the female role that historical civilizations have sculpted in line with their arranged organization; the male's historical and contemporary roles are no less bounded by the strictly delimited operations which sustain civilization. Though males have had comparatively broader options, none of these cogs in "a man's world" have allowed a full blossoming to all of his native equipment.

THE EFFECT OF LATENT POTENTIAL
ON SELF-IDENTITY

While today's world cushions us from barbarities that we can barely imagine, the fact is that in being "cushy," it is an insufficient task-master in calling forth much of human potentiality. On the other hand, it's obvious that in not exercising these potentials, none of us is prevented from surviving in the modern world. What I have tried to show is precisely that the modern world makes some of these capacities irrelevant, and thus keeps them as mere potentials. Furthermore, due to the pervasive competitiveness in modern societies this unseen element of human nature is not readily nor widely acknowledged.

Nevertheless its existence registers inside each person's own mind. No, the latent potential doesn't disappear, even when it remains unactualized. It becomes a driving force that generates an ideal image which makes up part of a person's identity. In the privacy of self-consciousness our innate potential, even when inert and unactualized, exerts a defining influence on the overall image we develop of ourselves. The presence of latent potential serves as raw material for the construction of an ideal self-image.

Of course, by itself, this neurological substrate of potential would probably remain completely dormant inside us. But there is something else that regularly acts like leavening which makes us fully conscious of its existence. Since at any given moment we are conscious of an impending future, the possibility of utilizing aspects of our potential always remains a conceivable option. There is always tomorrow and the day after tomorrow, and all the possibilities commensurate with this.

Taken together the idealized sense of self which is an integral aspect of our identities takes form from the push exerted by our unactualized potentials, and the pull received from a future filled with viable possibilities. In order to reconcile these two palpable realities, those who have not given up on themselves hold an image of themselves which represents what they may yet be able to do. This image is the self-ideal.

* * *

The self-ideal is based on an autonomous appraisal of one's own latent capacities. It is a personified image of ways in which these capacities might be enacted. At the same time, this is why the clinical view of this matter has it backwards. Among most people what engenders love is not a back door assuagement of their sense of unworthiness, but precisely the opposite condition of our *corroborating* certain capacities which usually go unacknowledged in this world.

And because a person's desire to somehow actualize their best-self is founded on an inner reservoir of deeply felt potentials, our validation of their self-ideal can have a visceral effect no less consummating than sex. We show them that the two worlds of ideal and real go together after all.

For seduction, this openness to the more positive side of another's character is indispensable. What love often, and seduction always needs, is someone who will take the initiative in validating another's best self.

257

NOTES

CHAPTER ONE
1. Francesco Alberoni, *Falling in Love* (New York: Random House, 1983), pp.72-73.
2. Heather T. Remoff, *Sexual Choice, A Woman's Decision* (New York: Dutton Lewis, 1984), p.xiv.

CHAPTER TWO
1. G. W. F. Hegel, *Philosophy of Right* (Oxford: Clarendon Press, 1945), p.261.
2. William James, *Principles of Psychology*, 2 vols. (New York: Henry Holt, 1890), vol.I p.306.

CHAPTER FOUR
1. Albert Ellis, *The Art and Science of Love* (New York: Lyle Stuart, Inc., 1960).
2. Rollo May, *The Meaning of Anxiety*, (New York: The Ronald Press Co., 1950).
3. Richard Sennett, *The Fall of Public Man* (New York: Random House, 1976).
4. Peter A. Bertocci, *The Person and Primary Emotions* (New York: Springer-Verlag, 1988).

CHAPTER FIVE
1. Stendhal (Henri Beyle), *De l'amour*, orig.ed.1822, P. Woolf & C. Woolf Trans. (New York: Brentano's, no date).
2. Magda B. Arnold, *Emotion and Personality* 2 vols. (New York: Columbia University Press, 1960).
3. Susanne K. Langer, *Mind: An Essay on Human Feeling* (Baltimore: The Johns Hopkins Press, 1967).

CHAPTER SIX
1. Theodor Reik, *The Need to be Loved* (New York: Farrar, Straus, 1963), p.65.

CHAPTER SEVEN
    1. Dorothy Tennov, *Love and Limerence* (New York: Stein and Day, 1979), p.54.
    2. Jose Ortega y Gasset, *Estudios Sobre El Amor* (Madrid: Revista de Occidente, S.A., 1939).

CHAPTER EIGHT
    1. Soren Kierkegaard, "Diary of the Seducer" in Robert Meister ed., *A Literary Guide to Seduction* (New York: Stein and Day, 1963), p.36.

CHAPTER NINE
    1. J. Simenauer & D. Carroll, *Singles, The New Americans* (New York: Simon and Schuster, 1982).
    2. Zick Rubin, *Liking and Loving* (New York: Holt, Rinehart and Winston, Inc. 1973).
    3. Yonima Talmon, "Mate Selection in Collective Settlements," *American Sociological Review*, 29:491-508, 1964.

CHAPTER ELEVEN
    1. C. S. Ford and F. A. Beach, *Patterns of Sexual Behavior* (New York: Harper & Brothers, 1951), p.101.
    2. Timothy Perper, *Sex Signals, The Biology of Love* (Philadelphia: ISI Press, 1985), p.127.
    3. Ibid., p.134.
    4. Helen Gurley Brown, *Sex and the Single Girl* (New York: Bernard Geis, 1962), p.83.

CHAPTER TWELVE
    1. William Novak, *The Great American Man Shortage* (New York: Rawson Associates, 1983).

CHAPTER THIRTEEN
    1. Janet T. Spence, "Gender Identity and Its Implications for the Concepts of Masculinity and Femininity," in Nebraska Symposium on Motivation: *Psychology and Gender* (University of Nebraska Press, 1984).
    2. Stephen M. Johnson, *First Person Singular* (New York: J.B. Lippincott, 1977), p.176.
    3. Sally Jessy Raphael, *Finding Love* (New York: Arbor House, 1984), p.207.

CHAPTER FOURTEEN
1. Theodor Reik, *Listening With The Third Ear* (New York: Farrar, Straus, 1948), p.480.
2. Georg Simmel, *The Sociology of Georg Simmel*, trans. & ed. by Kurt H. Wolff (New York: Free Press, 1950), p.126.
3. Carl Gustav Jung, *Psychological Types* (New York: Harcourt, Brace, 1924).
4. Gardner Murphy, *Personality* (New York: Harper & Brothers, 1947), pp.596-597.
5. Henry Murray, *Explorations in Personality* (New York: Oxford University Press, 1938), p.215.

CHAPTER FIFTEEN
1. Hans Jurgen Eysenck, *Dimensions of Personality* (London: Routledge, Kegan, Paul, 1947), pp.246-247.
2. Henry Murray, *Explorations in Personality* (New York: Oxford University Press, 1938), p.212.
3. John Cowper Powys, *The Meaning of Culture* (New York: W. W. Norton, 1929), p.226.
4. Abraham Maslow, *Motivation and Personality* second ed. (New York: Harper & Row, 1970), p.192.
5. J. C. Powys, Ibid., p.145.
6. H. J. Eysenck, *Sense and Nonsense in Psychology* (Baltimore: Penguin, 1957), p.263.

CHAPTER SIXTEEN
1. William McDougall, *Outline of Psychology* (New York: Scribners, 1923), p.353.
2. H. G. Wells, *The Anatomy of Frustration* (New York: Macmillan, 1936), pp.172, 173, 194, 195.
3. Kahlil Gibran, *The Prophet* (New York: Knopf, 1923), p.16.
4. Wells, Ibid., pp.166, 168.

CHAPTER EIGHTEEN
1. Else Frenkel-Brunswik, "Intolerance of Ambiguity as an Emotional and Perceptual Personality Variable," in *Else Frenkel-Brunswik: Selected Papers*, N. Heiman & J. Grant, eds. (New York: International Universities Press, Inc., 1974), p.83.

2. Gordon W. Allport, *Personality* (New York: Henry Holt and Company, 1937).

3. The basic idea developed in this chapter occurred to me twenty years ago while applying Wilhelm Dilthey's method of psychography to the description of moral styles contained in William E. H. Lecky's treatment of moral development in European history. Subsequently, I found a corroborating perspective contained in Barton Perry's opus on values. *c.f.:*
Wilhelm Dilthey, *Pattern and Meaning in History,* H. P. Riekman, ed. (London: Allen & Unwin, Ltd., 1961).
William E. H. Lecky, *History of European Morals* 2 vols. (New York: D. Appleton and Company, 1897).
Ralph B. Perry, *General Theory of Value* (New York: Longmans, Green and Company, 1926).

CHAPTER NINETEEN

1. Glenn D. Wilson, "The Concept of Conservatism" in *The Psychology of Conservatism,* G. D. Wilson, ed. (London: Academic Press, 1973).

2. William E.H. Lecky, *The Map of Life* (London: Longmans, Green and Company, 1899), p.58.

3. Bernard I. Murstein, "A Theory of Marital Choice and Its Applicability to Marriage Adjustment," in *Theories of Attraction and Love,* B. I. Murstein, ed. (New York: Springer Publishing Company, Inc., 1971), p.116.

4. Benjamin Spock, *Decent and Indecent* (New York: The McCall Publishing Company, 1969).

5. Charles Hampden-Turner, *Radical Man* (Garden City: Anchor Books, 1971).

6. R. B. Cattell, *Description and Measurement of Personality* (Yonkers: World Book Co., 1946).

APPENDIX

1. Plato, *The Dialogues of Plato* 4 vols. B. Jowett Trans. (New York: Bigelow Brown, 1914), vol.3 p.315, vol.4 p.363.

The symbolical image Plato chose to portray this state of togetherness was of a being made up of two parts: his view of our species ancestors as being physically joined in pairs was an intuitive foreshadow of what we now refer to as the group mind. Somehow Plato sensed that early homosapiens experienced life collectively, without the prison given to it by our subsequently developed individuality. This phylogenetic conceptualization has been more elaborately worked out by Sir Arthur Keith in his, *A New Theory of Human Evolution* (New York: Philosophical Library, 1949); and more recently by Michael S. Gazzaniga in his, *The Social Brain* (New York: Basic Books, 1985).

2. Erich Fromm, *The Art of Loving* (New York: Harper & Row, 1956), pp.7, 17.

3. Rene Descartes, "The Passions of the Soul," in *The Philosophical Works of Descartes* 2 vols. (London: Cambridge University Press, 1970), vol.1 p.371.

4. Richard Centers, *Sexual Attraction and Love, An Instrumental Theory* (Springfield: Charles C. Thomas, 1975), p.69.

5. Stendhal, *De l'amour*, orig.ed.1822, P. Woolf & C. Woolf Trans. (New York: Brentano's, no date).

6. S. Freud, *Group Psychology and the Analysis of the Ego* (New York: Liveright, 1940), p.56.

7. Theodor Reik, *Of Love and Lust* (New York: Grove, 1959), pp.16, 18.

8. Robert F. Winch, *The Modern Family* (New York: Holt, 1952). Also see Winch's *Mate Selection* (New York: Harper, 1958) and T. Ktsanes & V. Ktsanes, "The Theory of Complementary Needs in Mate Selection" in R. Winch, R. McGinnis, H. Barringer, eds. *Selected Studies in Marriage and The Family* (New York: Holt, Rinehart and Winston, 1962).

9. Morton M. Hunt, "How Do We Choose a Mate?" in *The Readers Digest*, 1959.

10. M. F. Nimkoff, Book Review, *American Journal of Sociology* January 1959 64:4 p.428.

11. Hunt, Ibid.

12. Robert H. Frank, *Passions Within Reason* (New York: W. W. Norton & Company, 1988).

13. Arthur Aron & Elaine N. Aron, *Love and the Expansion of Self* (New York: Hemisphere Publishing Corporation, 1986).

14. Herbert Spencer, *Principles of Psychology* 2 vols. (New York: D. Appleton, 1896), vol.1 p.487.

15. Spencer, Ibid.

16.   Robert J. Sternberg, "A Triangular Theory of Love," *Psychological Review*, 93:119-135, 1986.

17.   Concepts cited on table are drawn from following works:

Ziek Rubin, *Liking and Loving* (New York: Holt, Rinehart and Winston, 1973).

Richard Centers *Sexual Attraction and Love, An Instrumental Theory*, (Springfield: Charles C. Thomas, 1975).

Glenn Wilson, *The Coolidge Effect* (New York: Morrow, 1981).

Willard Gaylin, *Rediscovering Love* (New York: Viking Penguin, 1986).

R.J. Sternberg, *The Triangle of Love* (New York: Basic Books, 1988).

P. Shaver, C. Hazan and D. Bradshaw, "Love as Attachment: The Integration of Three Behavioral Systems," in R. Sternberg and M. Barnes, eds. *The Psychology of Love* (New Haven: Yale University Press, 1988).

18.   Centers, *Sexual Attraction and Love* p.87. Also see: Centers R. and Granville A. C., "Reciprocal need gratification in intersexual attraction: A Test of the hypothesis of Schutz and Winch," *Journal of Personality*, 39:26-43, 1971.

Centers, R. "Evaluating the loved one: the motivational congruency factor," *Journal of Personality*, 39:303-318, 1971.

19.   Theodore H. Blau, "The Love Effect" in H. A. Otto, *Love Today* (New York: Delta, 1972), pp.154, 155.

20.   Blau, Ibid., p.157.

21.   Theodor Reik, *A Psychologist Looks at Love* (New York: Holt, Rinehart and Winston, 1944), p.61.

22.   T. Reik, "The Chip on the Shoulder," in Hilda Holland ed. *Why are You Single?* (New York: Farrar Straus, 1949), pp.5, 6, 10.

23.   T. Reik, Ibid. *A Psychologist Looks at Love*, pp.49, 50.

24.   Franz J. Kallman, "The Genetics of Human Behavior," *American Journal of Psychiatry* 113:496-501, 1956.

25.   Julian Jaynes, *The Origin of Consciousness in the Breakdown of the Bicameral Mind* (Boston: Houghton Mifflin, 1976), p.130.

26.   J. N. Spuhler, "Somatic Paths to Culture," in *The Evolution of Man's Capacity for Culture*, arranged by J. N. Spuhler (Detroit: Wayne State University Press, 1959).

27.   Harry J. Jerison, "The Evolution of Consciousness," in *Mind and Brain*, Sir John Eccles, ed. (New York: Paragon House Publishers, 1985).

INDEX

acceptance, 125, 139
admiration, 124, 130, 196
affair, 128
affectionate, 131
affinity, 89, 117, 136, 137, 156
affirmation, 56, 65, 68, 69, 70,
    74, 76, 179
Alberoni F., 14, 259
Allport, G., 262
ambivalence, 184, 185
anonymity, 115
anticipation, 71, 137, 138
anxiety, 86, 225
aphrodisiac, 111
appearance, 59, 63, 122, 155
Appetite for Pleasure, 74-75, 211,
    212-214
approval, 68, 139, 169, 198
Aristophanes, 225
Arnold, M., 259
Aron, Arthur & Elaine, 239
assumptions, 92, 130, 242
attachment, 148, 170, 211
attention, 71-75, 150
attitude toward responsibility, 188,
    190-92, 193
attraction, 13, 43, 70, 76, 83, 84,
    92, 118, 122, 151, 227
Authentic Preference, 81-85, 95,
    97-98, 211
authenticity, 219
availability, 105, 136

Beach, F. A., 110, 260
Bertocci, P. A., 259
Beyle, Henri, see Stendahl
biological programming, 60, 61,
    109, 251-53
blank slate, 90-92
Blau, T., 246, 264
blowing hot and cold, 71-74
bohemian, 193, 202
"breaking the ice", 96-97
    with males, 109-12
    with females, 113-17
brief separations, 73, 74
Brown, H. G., 260

business, 17, 62, 168

Carnegie, Dale, 27
Carroll, D., 260
Cattel, R. B., 202, 262
Centers, R., 227, 243, 244, 264-65
challenges, 156, 157, 185-87
character, 191, 199
"chemistry", 122, 127, 137
chivalry, 120
closeness, 67, 150, 151, 160, 171, 181
coincidence, 95, 96, 211
commitment, 107, 109, 163, 178,
    186, 244
compatibility, 136
complimentary union, 170, 235,
    236, 237
compliments, 189
confirmation, 42, 66, 68, 124, 126,
    127, 167, 226
congeniality, 152
conservatives, 190, 191, 193,
    195-99
control, 152-54, 191, 195
conventional, 188, 192, 198
conversation, 67, 114-16, 136, 139, 180
courtesy, 198
Croft, R., 51
Crystallization, 228-30
curiosity, 117, 214-16
Dating, 97, 127-28, 129, 136, 178, 234
daydream, 147, 155
decision, 121, 186
defense mechanisms, 66, 185
deliberate overture, 89
deliberate determination, 163, 175
demands, 186, 187
demographics, 87, 103
dependability, 196
Descartes, Rene, 225-26, 230, 263
desire, 70, 71, 123, 127, 157, 161,
    213, 257
Dilthey, W., 262
directness, 195
doubts, 75

ego, 66, 137, 158, 161, 218, 219, 232, 247
eligible men, 103, 109
Ellis, Albert, 42, 259
embarrassed, 115
emotion, 30, 41, 60-64, 136, 165, 183
emotional rapport, 48, 136, 145,
    149, 155, 157, 166, 176
empathy, 37, 160
enchantment, 207, 209, 210, 211,
    214, 215, 216
encouragement, 167, 169
enjoyment, 213, 214
enthusiasm, 162
erotic arousal, 42, 56
etiquette, 110, 199
expectations, 105, 117, 120, 121,
    128-31, 179, 212, 213, 214
extrovert, 48, 138, 141, 142-45,
    153, 160, 163, 164-82, 193
eye contact, 109, 111, 113
Eysenck, H., 147, 155, 160, 261

falling in love, 8, 14-15, 51, 55,
    58, 71, 117, 135, 183-88
familiarity, 91
fantasy, 155
Fate, 13, 14, 55, 89, 105, 211
fated encounters, 120
feedback, 166, 169, 170, 174, 176, 181
feminine, 17, 41, 62, 111, 124
finding someone, 94-99
finesse, 115
first impression, 88, 122, 123, 139
flexibility, 108
flirting, 131
Ford, C. S., 110, 260
foreknowledge, 7, 13, 20, 37, 56,
    64, 108, 206
Frank, R. H., 263
Frenkel-Brunswick, E., 190, 261
Freud, S., 44, 232-235, 247
friends, 115, 148, 160, 176, 198
Fromm, E., 225, 239, 263
future, 161, 256

Gaylin, W., 243
Gazzaniga, M. S., 263
gender identity, 16-18, 40-43, 120,
    121-27, 136, 183, 187, 226-27
Gibran, Kahlil, 171, 173, 261
Goethe, 192, 195, 196

gratitude, 70

Hampden-Turner, C., 262
health club, 125
heart & mind, conjunction of, 20
Hegel G. F., 23, 259
heterosexual, 17, 40
Hollywood, 83
homosexual relations, 40
hope, 22, 37, 39, 74, 109, 161, 216
Howarth, V., 101
Hunt, M., 238, 239

idealization, see Crystallization
ideological outlook, 190, 194, 200
illusion, 159, 224, 246
imagination, 155, 227, 228, 245
imitation, 213
impressionable, 165
impulsive, 165, 166, 212
inaccessibility, 148, 154
incompatibility, 129
Individuality, 23, 170, 171, 173-74,
    176, 180, 215
infatuation, 39, 76
ingratiate, 66, 167
initial attitude, 86-90, 92, 97-99
innovativeness, 201, 202, 204
intelligence, 28, 122, 136
intentions, 96, 97-98, 113, 189
intimacy, 44, 46, 67, 68, 139, 141
introvert, 48, 138, 141, 142-45,
    147-63, 170, 176, 193
intuition, 61, 204, 205
invitations, 128
involvement, 137, 139, 186
irreplaceable, 177-80

James, William, 30, 31, 38, 259
Jaynes, J., 264
Jerison, H. J., 264
Johnson, S. M., 260
judgments, 121, 140, 142, 171,
    188, 205
Jung, C. G., 141, 148, 165, 166,
    167, 261

Kallman, F. J., 264
Kama Sutra, 220
Kierkegaard, S., 53, 84, 260
Keith, A., 263

Kibbutz, 91
Ktsanes, T. & V., 263

Langer, S. K., 259
latent potential, 49, 50, 249-55
Lecky, W. E. H., 262
liberals, 190, 191, 193, 200-06
lifestyle, 106, 107, 136, 190
loneliness, 47, 172, 173
Love,
    as cosmic force, 16, 224
    as mode of fulfillment, 32-36,
        55, 229
    causes, 7, 15, 50, 62
    components, 8, 16, 28, 240,
        241-45
    concepts of, 224-245
    subjective sense of, 23,
        25-27, 61, 63, 133, 210
    unconscious, and, 58, 59, 60,
        67, 76, 128, 138, 218,
        229-30, 234-35, 244
loyalty, 198
Luck, 13, 58, 88, 153

machismo, 17
Markham, E., 79
marriage, 91, 92, 112, 129, 161, 179, 240
masculine, 41, 114, 124, 125
Maslow, A., 158, 159, 161, 162, 261
mate selection, 235-38
mating patterns, 47, 110
May, R., 44, 259
McDougall, W., 166, 261
merging, 89, 159, 160, 173
mind-set, 72, 148, 150, 164, 167
motives, 44, 56, 81, 97, 224, 234,
    236, 239
Murphy, G., 143, 261
Murray, H., 144, 148, 261
Murstein, B., 197, 262
mystery, 11, 55, 92, 105

National Institute of Mental Health, 236
neediness, 57, 81
Nietzsche, 27
Nimkoff, M. F., 263
"no fault", 87, 90
nonchalance, 124, 127
nonverbal cues, 109-12
Novak, W., 260

novelty, 91, 92, 131, 166

opinion, 116, 144
opposite sex, 41, 226
opposites, 170
optimistic, 125, 130
Ortega y Gasset, 71, 72, 207, 210,
    239, 260
overture, 89, 98, 109, 111, 127
Ovid, 5

Passion, 18, 49, 70, 73, 103, 131,
    197, 206, 217
passive, 25, 110, 114
permanence, 146
Perper, T., 110, 111, 260
Perry, R. B., 262
persistence, 97-99, 105
Person, E. S., 133
persona, 167, 203
personality types, see introverts
    & extroverts and conventional
    & unconventional
pickup, 111, 115
Plato, 224-25, 230, 262
pleasure, 212, 213, 229
poise, 97
Powys, J. C. 148, 159, 167, 261
predispositions, see emotion
preoccupation, 72, 75, 104, 105,
    137, 149, 168
priorities, 103, 104
Proceptivity - see nonverbal cues
professional women, 104

Raphael, S. J., 260
readiness, 90
reciprocation, 125, 153
Reik, T., 66, 137, 228, 233, 247-48, 259
rejection, 88, 98, 139
reliability, 197
reluctance, 139, 178
Remoff, H., 16, 17, 259
reputation, 24, 25
response chord, 50, 59, 62, 109, 230
responsibility, 88
restraint, 123
rewards, 218-20
roles, 24, 29, 40, 41, 111, 114, 117,
    118, 123, 125, 176, 227

romance, 40, 41, 58, 117, 118, 120, 124, 129, 206
romantic atmosphere, 92, 131
romantic mood, 136-37, 140, 155
Rubin, Z., 243, 260

secretive, 37, 66
seduction defined, 21, 56-57, 62, 63, 101, 136
self-blame, 88, 107-08
self-consciousness, 116, 147
self-esteem, 168, 241, 244, 245
self-estimate, 50, 210
self-feelings, 29-30, 35, 64, 66, 139, 169, 198, 218
self-fulfilling prophecy, 104, 130
self-ideal, 49-51, 183, 186-88, 189-94, 194-206, 228-30, 244, 245-57
self-identity, 15, 16, 18, 67,174, 194, 250
self-image, 28, 49, 65, 92, 140, 189, 203
self-respect, 167
self-worth, 23-25, 28-29, 58, 63, 66
selfless, 11, 218, 239
Sennett, R., 259
sense of belonging, 46, 47, 48, 107, 141, 146, 151, 163
sensitivity, 66-69, 75, 152, 168, 212
sentiments, 143, 144, 149, 150, 154, 158, 162, 164
sex appeal, 122
sex, 42, 44, 46, 232-34
Shakespeare, 53
shared needs, 158-62
shared sympathies, 148, 149, 150, 151
Shaver, P., 243
Shaw, G. B., 191, 192
Simenauer, J., 260
Simmel, G., 141, 261
singles bars, 96, 110
singles, 82, 87, 94, 103
social impulse, 43, 140
social identity, 43-48, 137, 138, 140, 146, 187, 229
Solomon, R., 11
Spence, J. T., 260
Spencer, H., 240, 241, 243
Spock, B., 262
Spuhler, J. N., 264
Stendahl, 59, 227-29, 230, 244, 259

stereotypes, 41, 83, 109, 113, 118, 126, 127
Sternberg, R. J., 243, 264
strangers, 92, 109, 114, 115, 118, 124, 149
strategy, 8, 15, 56, 69, 70-76, 81, 209, 214
stress, 191, 194, 195
subjectivity, 143, 148, 149, 156, 158, 178
sublimation, 44
Sullivan, H. S., 174
surrender, 196, 197
symbolical, 8, 204, 232, 250

Talmon, Y., 260
tastes, 159, 160
temperament, 126, 149, 190, 191, 192, 193
temptation, 84
Tennov, D., 70, 260
"testing the water", 96-97
trust, 197, 212
trustworthiness, 196, 197, 212

unavailable 98
uncertainty, 70, 74
unconventional, 188, 202-04
uniqueness, 175-77, 180
unpredictable, 88, 105

validation, 24, 48, 56, 127, 183, 187, 188, 189, 194, 195-206, 257
values, 136, 190, 192, 197, 206
Victorian period, 44, 232
virility, 41
virtues, 36, 195, 196

Waldenbooks Romance Club, 117
way of relating, 138-40, 170
Wells, H. G., 167, 168, 169, 172,
Whitehead, A. N., 221
Wilson, G., 243, 264
Winch, R. F., 235-38, 239, 240, 241

zero-sum game, 36, 104, 105
zest, 74, 75, 213, 214